LiveCode Mobile Development Beginner's Guide
Second Edition

Create interactive mobile apps for Android and iOS with LiveCode

Colin Holgate

Joel Gerdeen

PUBLISHING

BIRMINGHAM - MUMBAI

LiveCode Mobile Development Beginner's Guide
Second Edition

First published: July 2012

Second published: May 2015

Production reference: 1250515

Published by Packt Publishing Ltd.
Livery Place
35 Livery Street
Birmingham B3 2PB, UK.

ISBN 978-1-84969-965-5

www.packtpub.com

Credits

Authors

Colin Holgate

Joel Gerdeen

Reviewers

Randy Hengst

Akinori Kinoshita

Jane Wilson

Commissioning Editor

Mary Nadar

Acquisition Editors

Vivek Anantharaman

Mary Nadar

Content Development Editor

Rohit Singh

Technical Editor

Aman Preet Singh

Copy Editor

Neha Vyas

Project Coordinator

Mary Alex

Proofreaders

Stephen Copestake

Safis Editing

Indexer

Monica Ajmera Mehta

Production Coordinator

Nilesh R. Mohite

Cover Work

Nilesh R. Mohite

About the Authors

Colin Holgate was originally trained as a telecommunications technician in the Royal Air Force, but with the advent of the personal computer era, he transitioned to working as a technical support engineer for companies, which included Apple Computers, UK.

In 1992, he moved to the US to become a full-time multimedia programmer working for The Voyager Company. In that role, he programmed several award-winning CD-ROMs, including A Hard Day's Night and This Is Spinal Tap.

For the last 17 years, Colin worked for Funny Garbage, a New York City-based web design company. In addition to using Adobe Director and Adobe Flash for online and kiosk applications, he has used LiveCode to create in-house and client production tools. At the RunRevLive Conference in 2011, Colin entered and won a contest to create a mobile application made with LiveCode.

Joel Gerdeen obtained a PhD in engineering mechanics and biomedical engineering from Iowa State University, where he started using computers in experimental research. In his first employment as a structural analyst, he developed software to assist other engineers to graphically model heavy machinery. His support of engineering computer usage transitioned into a career of software project management at FMC, Honeywell, and BAE Systems, all of which were Fortune 100 companies. Joel has experienced computing evolution from loading machine code through switches on a DEC minicomputer to booting a Raspberry Pi from a microSD card. He has worked with microprocessors, timesharing, personal computers, mainframe business systems, and latest mobile devices.

After 35 years of employment, Joel ventured into mobile software development in 2010, working with a small start-up company and publishing numerous apps on both Apple and Google app stores. After working with separate iOS and Android development environments, he discovered LiveCode and was able to build on his former HyperCard experience. Joel is also active in the mobile development community in Minneapolis and has presented LiveCode at local conferences.

I would like to thank the LiveCode staff and all its active users who have provided a treasure trove of experience through examples, lessons, and discussion groups. I'd like to especially thank the original author, Colin Holgate, for the first edition that helped me learn LiveCode and for the experience I gained in coauthoring this edition.

About the Reviewers

Randy Hengst is a long time educator. He began his career in 1975 as a 6th grade science teacher and subsequently taught 4th grade. He has also worked as a building-level administrator in middle and elementary schools. He was a middle school assistant principal when the first Apple II lab was placed in the school building. As an elementary principal, he helped a handful of 6th grade students learn to use HyperCard. He earned a PhD in 1990 and has worked as a teacher since 1993 at Augustana College, Rock Island, IL. There, he introduced the teacher candidates to scripting within HyperCard and HyperStudio. His current projects are all developed with LiveCode for iOS and are designed to support a collaborative program with a local elementary school, the Number Sense Project. In this project, elementary education majors work with college faculty and kindergarten teachers to design and implement lessons designed to facilitate the kindergarteners' sense of numbers. The elementary education majors and kindergarten teachers regularly make suggestions to create new and modify existing apps. Refer to the apps at `http://www.classroomfocusedsoftware.com/numbersense.html`. Also, you can read more about the Number Sense Project at `http://www.augustana.edu/numbersense/index.htm`.

Akinori Kinoshita holds a bachelor's degree in electrical engineering from Purdue University and a master's degree in business administration from National Taiwan University. Besides his work, he actively participates in the free, libre, and open source software (FLOSS) art movement. He takes workshops on Processing, (fluxus), and SuperCollider for artists and nonprogrammers in Taipei, Taiwan.

I would like to thank my father, mother, and sisters for their support. Without them, I wouldn't be here.

Jane Wilson is a web developer with a master's degree in user experience engineering and a bachelor's degree in applied computing from University of Dundee. Currently working in Dundee, she also writes for Geek Scot, a technology news site focused on Scotland.

www.PacktPub.com

Support files, eBooks, discount offers, and more

For support files and downloads related to your book, please visit www.PacktPub.com.

Did you know that Packt offers eBook versions of every book published, with PDF and ePub files available? You can upgrade to the eBook version at www.PacktPub.com and as a print book customer, you are entitled to a discount on the eBook copy. Get in touch with us at service@packtpub.com for more details.

At www.PacktPub.com, you can also read a collection of free technical articles, sign up for a range of free newsletters and receive exclusive discounts and offers on Packt books and eBooks.

https://www2.packtpub.com/books/subscription/packtlib

Do you need instant solutions to your IT questions? PacktLib is Packt's online digital book library. Here, you can search, access, and read Packt's entire library of books.

Why subscribe?

- ◆ Fully searchable across every book published by Packt
- ◆ Copy and paste, print, and bookmark content
- ◆ On demand and accessible via a web browser

Free access for Packt account holders

If you have an account with Packt at www.PacktPub.com, you can use this to access PacktLib today and view 9 entirely free books. Simply use your login credentials for immediate access.

Table of Contents

Preface

Everyone you know has a smart mobile device of some kind. You probably own several too! The general idea of having utility applications on a phone is not new. Even cell phone and PDA games have existed for years, but the way that iPhone used touch instead of a stylus or keyboard and the way it used gestures to reduce the number of steps to do something was a game changer.

iPhone was released in June 2007 and the Android OS was released in September 2008. If you wanted to create something that worked on both platforms, you'd had to learn two development environments and languages: Objective-C for iPhone and Java for Android.

In the desktop world, there are several development tools that allow you to publish apps on both Mac and Windows as well as Linux in the case of LiveCode. The most successful of these tools are Adobe Director, Adobe Flash, Unity, and LiveCode. Publishing apps to iOS was introduced with Adobe Director 12, which means that all four tools are also suitable for mobile development.

These tools have different strengths; in some cases, the strengths relate to the nature of the applications you can make and in other cases, they relate to how accessible the tool is to people who are not hardcode programmers. If you want to make a high-quality 3D game, Unity would be the best choice, with Director and then Flash as other choices. If you need a lot of character animations, Flash would be the best choice, Adobe Director being a good alternate.

If the most important thing for you is how approachable the tool is, then LiveCode wins easily. It's also a valid choice to make the majority of apps you might wish to make. In fact, for apps that are a set of single screens, as would be the case for most utility apps as well as board and puzzle games, LiveCode is better suited than other tools. It also has better access to native interface elements; with the other tools, you usually have to create graphics that resemble the look of native iOS and Android controls instead of accessing the real thing.

With its easy-to-use near-English programming language and the stack of cards metaphor, LiveCode lets you concentrate more on creating the app you want to make and less on the technicalities of the development environment.

What this book covers

Chapter 1, LiveCode Fundamentals, introduces you to the LiveCode environment and to its near-English programming language. Experienced LiveCode users can skip this chapter, but for someone new to LiveCode, this chapter will take you through the process of creating a simple calculator app as a way to make you familiar with the various tools and hierarchy of LiveCode.

Chapter 2, Getting Started with LiveCode Mobile, describes in detail how to set up your Mac or Windows computer so that you are ready to develop and publish mobile apps. This chapter will take you all the way through from signing up as an iOS and Android developer to creating and testing your first LiveCode mobile app.

Chapter 3, Building User Interfaces, shows how to use some of the standard mobile features, such as date pickers, photo albums, and a camera. This chapter will also show you how to make your own buttons that have an iOS-like look to them and how to use the LiveCode add-on, MobGUI, to make your life easier!

Chapter 4, Using Remote Data and Media, discusses the structure of your apps, where to place your code, and how to read and write to external text files. Here, we will also create a mobile app that is a "web scraper" capable of extracting links and media from a web page to show or play media from that page.

Chapter 5, Making a Jigsaw Puzzle Application, will show you how to process image data and how to use the information to create a color picker, detect regions, and to make a collision map. We will then create a full jigsaw puzzle application that takes its image from the photo album or device camera.

Chapter 6, Making a Reminder Application, examines which information is needed to represent a "reminder" and how to set up notification events so that you are alerted at a specified date and time. Here, we will make a reminder app that can create a list of such events and even list those events based on your current location.

Chapter 7, Deploying to Your Device, is a reference chapter that describes all of the mobile publishing settings. This chapter also shows you how to send apps to beta testers and how to get started with the submission of your finished app to various app stores.

Appendix, Extending LiveCode, describes add-ons to LiveCode that will make your mobile apps look better or will extend the mobile capabilities of LiveCode. The planned LiveCode builder and widget capabilities of LiveCode's Version 8 are introduced as well.

What you need for this book

In addition to Community LiveCode 7.0 or its later versions, you will need a Mac or PC, iOS and/or Android devices, and some money if you follow the parts about signing up as a mobile developer in this book! For iOS development, you will need access to a Mac OS for some of the steps and these steps also require it to be an Intel-based Mac.

Who this book is for

The ideal reader for this book would be someone who already knows LiveCode, is interested in creating mobile apps, and wants to save the many hours it took for me to track down all of the information on how to get started! *Chapter 1, LiveCode Fundamentals*, will help those of you who know programming but are not familiar with LiveCode. The knowledge you've acquired should be enough for you to benefit from the remainder of the book.

Sections

In this book, you will find several headings that appear frequently (Time for action, What just happened?, Pop quiz, and Have a go hero).

To give clear instructions on how to complete a procedure or task, we use these sections as follows:

Time for action – heading

1. Action 1
2. Action 2
3. Action 3

The instructions here often need some extra explanation to ensure that they make sense, so they are followed with the following sections.

What just happened?

This section explains the working of the tasks or instructions that you have just completed.

You will also find some other learning aids in the book. Take the following section for example.

Pop quiz – heading

These are short multiple-choice questions intended to help you test your own understanding.

Have a go hero – heading

These are practical challenges that give you ideas to experiment with what you have learned.

Conventions

You will also find a number of text styles that distinguish between different kinds of information. Here are some examples of these styles and an explanation of their meaning.

Code words in text are shown as follows: "The contents of the display field are stored in the `currentValue` variable and the last operator button you pressed (that is stored in `currentCommand`) is looked at, to see what happens next."

A block of code is set as follows:

```
on togglesign
   if character 1 of field "display" is "-" then
     delete character 1 of field "display"
   else
     put "-" before field "display"
   end if
end togglesign
```

Any command-line input or output is written as follows:

```
start using stack "utility stack"
```

New terms and **important words** are shown in bold. Words that you see on the screen, in menus or dialog boxes for example, appear in the text like this: "In the **Tools** palette, click on the **Edit** tool (the top-right icon)."

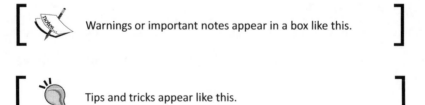

Warnings or important notes appear in a box like this.

Tips and tricks appear like this.

Reader feedback

Feedback from our readers is always welcome. Let us know what you think about this book—what you liked or disliked. Reader feedback is important for us as it helps us develop titles that you will really get the most out of.

To send us general feedback, simply e-mail feedback@packtpub.com, and mention the book's title in the subject of your message.

If there is a topic that you have expertise in and you are interested in either writing or contributing to a book, see our author guide at www.packtpub.com/authors.

Customer support

Now that you are the proud owner of a Packt book, we have a number of things to help you to get the most from your purchase.

Downloading the example code

You can download the example code files from your account at http://www.packtpub.com for all the Packt Publishing books you have purchased. If you purchased this book elsewhere, you can visit http://www.packtpub.com/support and register to have the files e-mailed directly to you.

Errata

Although we have taken every care to ensure the accuracy of our content, mistakes do happen. If you find a mistake in one of our books—maybe a mistake in the text or the code—we would be grateful if you could report this to us. By doing so, you can save other readers from frustration and help us improve subsequent versions of this book. If you find any errata, please report them by visiting http://www.packtpub.com/submit-errata, selecting your book, clicking on the **Errata Submission Form** link, and entering the details of your errata. Once your errata are verified, your submission will be accepted and the errata will be uploaded to our website or added to any list of existing errata under the Errata section of that title.

To view the previously submitted errata, go to https://www.packtpub.com/books/content/support and enter the name of the book in the search field. The required information will appear under the **Errata** section.

Piracy

Piracy of copyrighted material on the Internet is an ongoing problem across all media. At Packt, we take the protection of our copyright and licenses very seriously. If you come across any illegal copies of our works in any form on the Internet, please provide us with the location address or website name immediately so that we can pursue a remedy.

Please contact us at `copyright@packtpub.com` with a link to the suspected pirated material.

We appreciate your help in protecting our authors and our ability to bring you valuable content.

Questions

If you have a problem with any aspect of this book, you can contact us at `questions@packtpub.com`, and we will do our best to address the problem.

1

LiveCode Fundamentals

Is this chapter for you?

LiveCode has an English-like programming language, a graphical development environment, and an easy-to-understand structural metaphor. When you create an application, you spend more time thinking about how to implement the different features and less about the complexities of the tool you are using. However, if you've never used LiveCode before, it's still going to be unfamiliar at first. This chapter is to bring you up to speed and make you ready for the later chapters that will require you to be more familiar with the terminology and features of this tool.

All of LiveCode is easy, but there are thousands of easy things to learn! Throughout the book, we will look at these things, that you can use for mobile applications in particular, but first, we should go over some of the basics.

In this chapter, we will:

- ◆ Become familiar with the LiveCode environment
- ◆ Investigate the hierarchy of a LiveCode "stack"
- ◆ Create a simple calculator application
- ◆ Learn about the many different interface controls

So, let's get on with it.

Background history and metaphors

Many development tools only present a programming language along with programming interfaces to system routines. Higher-level tools often present the same things, but structured in such a way that it is possible to come up with real-world metaphors for the different aspects of the tool. LiveCode is very much like that, and its metaphor is a stack of cards. This metaphor originated with Apple Computer's HyperCard authoring tool, which was created by Bill Atkinson in the mid-1980s. The first version of HyperCard was released in August 1987 and it became a huge hit in both education and multimedia sectors. Companies such as The Voyager Company, published its entire product line which was created using HyperCard.

Other companies produced tools that were very much like HyperCard, but they also tried to give the user more features than were in HyperCard. The most prominent of these tools were SuperCard, Plus, and MetaCard. Plus went on to have an interesting life; the product itself became Windows-only (it was cross-platform at first), but later, the same code ended up in the Oracle Media Objects cross-platform tool. All of these tools perpetuated the metaphor of a stack of cards.

MetaCard was most notable for the fact that it was multiplatform and not just cross platform. *Stacks* is the general term used for documents created by these tools, made with MetaCard that ran on Unix and Linux systems, as well as Mac and Windows. Alas, it was somewhat ugly! The Scottish company RunRev made a product that attempted to present MetaCard in a more appealing way. Eventually, RunRev acquired MetaCard, and since 2003, RunRev has continued to build upon MetaCard using the product name Runtime Revolution, which was later renamed as LiveCode.

In March 2015, RunRev also changed the company name to LiveCode Ltd. This book has many references to `http://runrev.com/`, and it should still be maintained as such. However, If you have a problem with a URL, substitute it with `http://livecode.com/` or do a search on the LiveCode website.

In 2013, RunRev had a successful Kickstarter campaign and raised £494k ($775k) to make LiveCode open source. Version 6.0 of LiveCode was released in April 2013 as the first open source version. This led to an active development cycle with close to 20 stable releases culminating in version 7.0 of LiveCode in October 2014. This edition of this book is based on the version 7.0 of LiveCode.

The highlights of version 7 include Unicode support, display resolution independence, stretchable graphics, hybrid apps using a new browser, Mac Cocoa support, Raspberry Pi support, 64-bit Linux support, and much more. You can read more about version 7 of LiveCode in the October 23, 2014 newsletter issue at `http://newsletters.livecode.com/october/issue180/`. All LiveCode newsletters are available under the **LiveCode Help** menu.

In 2014, RunRev had another financing campaign to raise support for HTML5 and raised an additional $395k. This capability and the version 8 of LiveCode with open language support are described further in *Appendix*, *Extending LiveCode*.

Under the HyperCard variation of the stack of cards metaphor, documents consist of the cards that hold buttons, fields, and bitmap graphics; backgrounds that hold a set of cards; and stacks that hold a set of backgrounds. LiveCode takes a slightly different approach and rather than having backgrounds that hold cards, it allows you to group any set of interface controls and set those to act as if they are background entities. These end up being more flexible, though slightly alien to people who have used HyperCard a lot.

Both HyperCard and LiveCode provide ways to extend the hierarchy further. You are able to link other stacks. To save time rewriting the same set of functions in every stack, you might choose to have a stack dedicated to these functions and you can add that stack to the `stackInUse` property using the following command:

```
start using stack "utility stack"
```

Additionally, you can write "externals", which are commands and functions written in the C language, which can extend LiveCode's abilities even further.

You do have LiveCode, don't you?

If you haven't yet installed LiveCode, go to `http://livecode.com/download` and download the Community Edition for your development platform. This version is open source and free to use. You will need to provide your name and e-mail which establishes a user account for LiveCode. At the time of writing this book, you also get a free App Design Kit that includes an introductory video and a mobile `app2market.livecode` template.

If you plan to buy Commercial LiveCode, read through `http://www.runrev.com/store/` to understand the many variations of licenses that are there. As a rough guide, based on the price at the time of writing this book, to create mobile applications that are free, the cost would be $99, and if you want to make apps that you could charge for, the cost would be $299. Additional levels of use and support are available at extra cost.

The two editions of LiveCode have a distinctive color scheme too, with the Commercial Edition using blue elements and the Community Edition using green elements.

Once you have downloaded the Community Edition or bought one of the commercial licenses, go ahead and launch it!

Learning the lay of the land

When you first open LiveCode, you are shown a Start Center window, which functions as a way to open recent documents, a list of links to forums and information to get started, or to view promotional information. There is no harm in keeping that window open, but if you do close it, you can reopen it from the **Help** menu. You can also use **Backdrop** by selecting it from the **View** menu to hide other application windows on your screen.

If you look at LiveCode for the first time, you will notice a toolbar at the top of the screen, just below the menu bar. Take note of the rightmost items, such as **Sample Stacks**, **Tutorials**, **Resources**, and **Dictionary**. These areas are filled with information that will help you to get started with LiveCode. **Dictionary** is something that you will use a lot, and just browsing through the entries will either answer your immediate question, or give you advanced information about issues you'll run into later.

The **Help** menu also provides access to **User Guide** and useful links to other information. Check the **User Guide** section to read in depth about the features mentioned here.

Online lessons

In addition to the resources you see inside LiveCode itself, there is a tremendous amount of information and a number of tutorials on the RunRev website. A good starting point would be `http://lessons.runrev.com/`.

This screenshot shows the windows and palettes that we're going to use for now as well as the document window, which is a simple calculator that we will build soon:

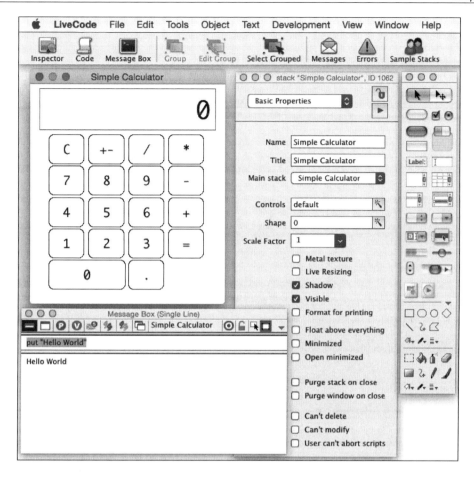

Main windows

In addition to the document window itself, these are the main windows that we need to be familiar with for now:

- ◆ Tools palette
- ◆ Inspector palette
- ◆ Message box

The upper area of the Tools Palette shows all the interface controls that you need to create an interactive application. Below these are a set of tools to edit vector graphics and a set of tools to edit bitmap graphics.

The Inspector Palette shows all the options for the control that you currently have selected. In the preceding screenshot, nothing is selected in the calculator app, so the Inspector Palette shows information about the stack itself.

Message Box is a window that lets you try out either single or multiple lines of code. You are able to invoke functions in your stacks too, making it a very handy way to test individual functions while you are tracking down issues. We'll use the Message Box in later chapters.

As suggested, read the User Guide to get a deeper understanding of these windows, but let's try putting together something simple for now to get you more familiar with how to use the Tool palette.

Time for action – it's a drag, but you'll like it!

You build things in LiveCode by dragging icons from the Tools palette to the stack window. If the palettes are not already open, the Inspector palette can be opened by clicking on the icon at the left end of the toolbar or by selecting one of the inspector menu items in the **Object** menu. The Tools palette can be opened by selecting the **Tools Palette** from the **Tools** menu and by using the following steps

1. From the **File** menu, select **New Mainstack**.

2. In the **Tools** palette, click on the **Edit** tool (the top-right icon).

To select edit or not...

In LiveCode, you can drag controls from the Tools palette to the card window without selecting the **Edit** tool. However, you are not able to select the control to adjust its position or size, and so, in the following instructions, we are intentionally selecting the **Edit** tool before adding controls to the card window:

1. Drag icons from the upper section of the Tools palette to the stack window.

2. Try the layering options at the bottom of the **Object** menu.

3. Select more than one item and experiment with the **Align Objects** options in the Inspector palette. The align options are shown automatically when you select multiple objects, but you can also select **Align Objects** from the drop-down menu in the Inspector palette. You won't see this option if only one object is selected. Here, we are able to see the options because three buttons are selected:

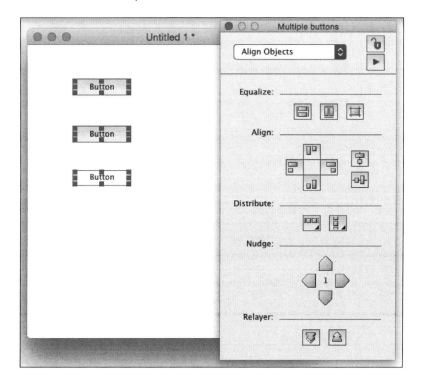

4. Select a single button and in the Inspector palette, enter a name and a label. If you don't see the **Name** and **Label** fields, make sure you have selected **Basic Properties** from the Inspector pallete's drop-down menu.

5. Add several more controls to the card window and practice aligning and naming the controls. You can also resize them by dragging the handles that you see on the corners and sides while the control is selected. Here is how the window would look if you add some buttons, a field, tab panel, slider, and video player control:

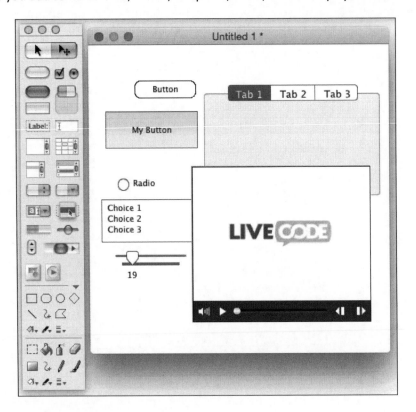

What just happened?

Hopefully, you will have made a random bunch of interface controls, perhaps some that are nicely lined up too! Now, select the **Close and Remove From Memory** option from the **File** menu and create a new **Main Stack** to make the Simple Calculator interface.

First though, we should go over some of the structure and hierarchy of a LiveCode stack and create some basic navigation.

Creating a hierarchy

Everything goes somewhere, but having things in the wrong place can lead to problems. We should learn more about the structure of a LiveCode stack to avoid this.

The stack structure

As described in the *Background history and metaphors* section, LiveCode uses a stack of cards metaphor. When you make a new stack, you in effect have a single stack of cards. However, even the simplest application is likely to have more than one card. For example, there could be a splash screen, title card, cards for the actual task at hand, and a credits page. In the calculator stack, we will use two cards. The **Tools** menu includes an option to view the structure of the stack by showing **Project Browser** or **Application Browser**. The Project Browser was introduced in the version 6.0 of LiveCode with additional capabilities

The Project Browser panel is a powerful tool that lets you see all the stacks, cards, and controls that are open at the moment, in one window. In addition to getting an overview of everything, you can use it as a remote control to jump between all the parts of your stack and to select and modify buttons, fields, and so on.

Taking the calculator stack that we are about to make as an example, in the following screenshot, we see a side-by-side view of the stack window and the Project Browser panel, where in the **Project Browser** panel, we have selected one of the buttons in the stack:

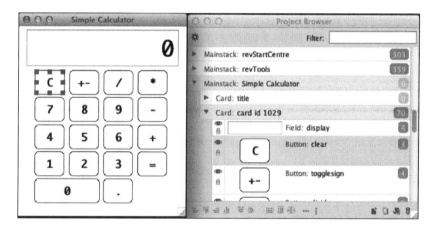

The upper area of **Project Browser** includes a field where you can type and search text to reduce the list of items in the browser to match the ones you have typed. In the upper-left part of the panel, is a gear icon that is used to take you to the preferences of the browser:

Most of the rest of the browser window lets you expand stacks and cards, and choose individual controls on those cards. Clicking on a control in **Project Browser** highlights it in the stack window and vice versa. Controls can also be reordered to change layers by dragging them up and down. Controls can also be hidden or locked by clicking on the eye and lock icons. The lower area buttons let you do various alignments of the selected controls to add or duplicate the selected control. Hovering over a button shows a popup of what it does.

A longer overview of how Project Browser works is available at:

http://www.runrev.com/newsletter/april/issue151/newsletter4.php.

Where does the code go?

In programming languages, such as the one in LiveCode, *code* is referred to as **scripts** and *methods* or *functions* are known as **handlers** (though in LiveCode, a handler that returns a value is also called a function). Projects made with hard-to-use programming tools often comprise dozens of external text files, one for each model, view, or controller. In LiveCode, this is simpler, as the scripts are attached to the object that needs that code.

To deal with user interaction in other tools, you will have to write code that receives the event (perhaps just a mouse click on a button) to perform the relevant action. In LiveCode, there is a message path that takes care of these events, and passes the event up the hierarchy. If you click on a LiveCode interface control that doesn't have a mouse event handler, the click goes up the hierarchy to the card level. If the card doesn't have a handler for that event, it continues up to the stack level.

You can have additional levels of hierarchy by putting other stacks in use, but for our purpose, we just need these three: the button, card, and stack.

This message hierarchy allows us to place the code needed via several interface controls at a higher level available to all of these controls. One case with the calculator number buttons is that each one needs to do exactly the same thing, and by putting that code in the card level, all of them can make use of that one handler.

There isn't a performance advantage if you have the shared handler in the card level or much of a file size improvement, but as you develop the code for the simple calculator example, you can make changes in the single-card script instead of the 11 calculator button scripts.

We will now start building the calculator and add scripts to the 14 buttons, a field, and the card.

Time for action – making cards and navigating between them

A calculator doesn't really need a title screen, but we'll make one anyway in order to practice adding scripts and to do some basic navigation. Start a new Mainstack from the **File** menu and open the **Inspector** palette.

1. In the **Inspector** palette, enter the Simple Calculator stack name in the **Name** field.

2. Select **New Card** from the **Object** menu.

3. Use the **View** menu to either go to the previous card (**Go Prev**) or first card (**Go First**).

4. Make sure you have the **Edit** tool selected in the **Tools** palette and drag a **Label** field to the middle of the card window. In this case, you can easily see which one is the **Label** field (it says **Label:** in the icon), but as a general tip, you can point to controls in the **Tools** Palette and see the help tip that shows what kind of control it is.

5. In the **Basic Properties** section of the **Inspector** palette, uncheck the **Don't wrap** checkbox.

6. Type `title` into the **Name** entry field.

7. Choose **Contents** from the **Inspector** drop-down menu and replace the initial text that says **Label:** by entering `Simple Calculator` into the **Contents** entry field.

8. Choose **Text Formatting** from the drop-down menu and click on the Align text center button, the middle of the three **Align** buttons.

9. Change the font, size, and style options to make a nice looking title, resizing the field itself until you like how it looks:

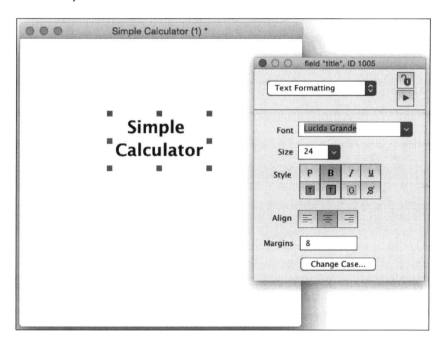

10. Drag a **Push** button (the second icon from the top-left corner of the **Tools** palette) from the **Tools** palette and place it below the title field.

11. In the **Inspector** palette, choose **Basic Properties** from the drop-down menu (it's the menu that says **Text Formatting** in the preceding screenshot) and enter `Begin` in the **Name** entry field. LiveCode will automatically show the same text as the button's label even though you didn't type it in the **Label** entry field.

12. You can go into the **Text Formatting** options for buttons too, if you wish!

13. Mentally prepare yourself; we're about to type in our first script!

14. With the button selected, choose **Object Script** from the **Object** menu. You can also right-click on the button itself and select **Edit Script**.

15. The script window will appear and show a starter script of `on mouseUp`, blank line, and `end mouseUp`, as shown in the following screenshot:

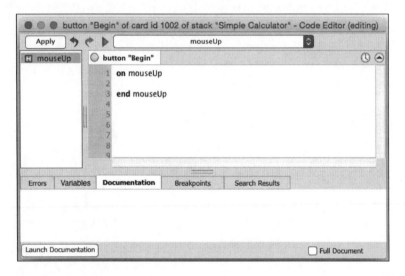

Complete the script by typing `go next` into the blank line to give you this final script:

```
on mouseup
   go next
end mouseup
```

Now, perform the following steps:

1. Close the script window and click on **Yes** when asked whether you want to save the changes.

2. Choose the **Browse** tool from the **Tools** palette (the upper leftmost tool that looks like a regular cursor arrow) and click on the **Begin** button that you just made. All being well, you're now looking at a blank card. Don't worry, you didn't just delete the title field and button! You're now on the second of the two cards that you made earlier. Use the **View** menu again to go back to the first card to try the button again.

3. Save! from the **File** menu, choose **Save** and save the stack with the `Simple Calculator` name somewhere you can easily find it later. Perhaps, you could make a folder to hold the several stacks you will make while reading this book.

What just happened?

These may have seemed like a lot of steps, but we did create the two cards we needed, laid out a nice looking title field, and a begin button with its own script. In reality, these steps take well under two minutes and will be even quicker to carry out as you gain experience in LiveCode.

Pop quiz – selecting the best name?

If you want to make it big in the multimedia authoring tool world, which of these names would be a bad choice?

1. Henry
2. Bill
3. Bob
4. Kevin

Answer: 1

In the early days of multimedia, it seemed like everyone had one of just a few popular names. There was Bill Atkinson, who created HyperCard, and Bill Appleton, who created SuperCard. Kevin Calhoun was the lead HyperCard programmer for a while and Kevin Miller is the head of LiveCode. Bob Stein was one of the founders of The Voyager Company and along with Bob Abel who was one of the pioneers in visual effects. Dan was another good choice as there was Dan Winkler, the author of the HyperTalk language, and Danny Goodman, the author of many famous programming books. Henry would be a good name if you wanted to make motorcars or marry lots of queens.

Making a simple calculator application

With even basic familiarity of LiveCode, you can start to make something of use. Here, we will make a very simple calculator stack.

Inspector clues, oh!

You will find yourself using the Inspector palette a lot; so, take a moment to study how it behaves. When you select an object on the card, you will see that the Inspector palette changes its appearance, sometimes even its height, to show the options for the item you have selected. It is smart enough to notice when you have selected multiple items and shows the align tools.

Sometimes, you will want to keep an Inspector palette set to view the options of a particular object on the card, and not switch so as to show a different object as you make other selections. In the upper-right corner of the Inspector palette is a padlock icon, which will let you lock the Inspector to the current object.

So far, most of the Inspector palette options haven't affected us, but one that is about to be relevant is the fact that you can set a name for an item that is different from its label. You may know from other programming languages, and this does apply to LiveCode too, that some names are less legal than others. Perhaps you can't have spaces in the name or use a colon or backslash. If you name a button with a number, button "1" may not be button 1 and this could lead to confusion.

For the calculator keys, we will set a label to make it look correct and a name that doesn't lead to confusion. Speaking of those calculator keys...

Time for action – making the calculator buttons

Using the screenshot shown at the start of this chapter as a guide, let's build the calculator buttons (the scripts you will type are also listed if you later want to make sure you typed them correctly):

1. If you're not already there, go to the second card, the currently empty one.
2. Make sure the **Edit** button is selected in the **Tools** palette and drag a **Push** button to the card, to the position of the 7 button.
3. In the **Basic Properties** panel of the Inspector palette, set the **Style** drop-down menu to **Rounded Rectangle** (in real life, you would take the time to have nice graphical buttons; here, you are just matching my ugly "programmer art"!).
4. Set the name of the button to number7 and the label to 7.

5. Select **Object Script** from the **Object** menu to see the starter script as you did with the **Begin** button.

6. In the empty line between `on mouseUp` and `end mouseUp`, type `numberPressed the label of me`. Note that `numberPressed` is a new handler that needs to be defined later. When used, `me` refers to the current object; in this case, the button pressed.

7. Close and save the script.

8. Select the button and make a copy of it by choosing **Duplicate Objects** from the **Edit** menu and position it where the **8** button will be. Copy/Paste and *Alt*-drag are two other ways to duplicate an object.

9. Set the name to `number8`, and label to `8`.

10. Repeat steps 8 and 9 for the buttons 9, 4, 5, 6, 1, 2, 3, 0, and the decimal point using the corresponding number instead of `8`. For the decimal point, let the name be `decimalpoint`.

11. Duplicate one of the buttons again, name the new button `divide`, and type / for its label.

12. Select `Object Script` for the divide button and change `numberPressed` in the middle line to say `operatorPressed`, making the whole line `operatorPressed the short name of me`.

13. Duplicate the divide button three more times and set the names to `multiply`, `plus`, and `minus`. Set the labels to `*`, `+`, and `-`.

14. Duplicate the divide button again, giving the new button a name `equals` and a label `=`, and change the middle line of script to say `equalsPressed`.

15. Duplicate the = button and set the new button's name to `toggleSign` and label to `+-`; then, change the middle line of script to `toggleSign`.

16. Duplicate the = button and set the new button's name to `clear` and label to `C`; then, change the middle line of script to be `clearPressed`.

17. Drag a **Label** field from the **Tools** palette and in the **Inspector** palette, choose `Text Formatting` from the drop-down menu. In the `Text Formatting` settings, choose a nice looking font, right-justified text, and a large font size. Name the field `display`.

18. Edit the script of the `display` field. With fields, you don't get the starter script that you get with buttons, so you will need to type the `mouseUp` lines yourself. Type these three lines in the script: `on mouseUp`, `set the clipboarddata["TEXT"] to me`, and `end mouseUp`. DO enter the quote marks on either side of the word `"TEXT"`.

19. Move all the buttons in their right spots and select the sets of buttons to then use the Align tools and make your calculator layout match the screenshot.

20. Save it now!

What just happened?

Quite a lot just happened! We have now made all the card level objects and typed in their scripts. Most of the scripts are "calling" up to a card level handler that we will be setting up next. Before doing that, it's worth trying to understand some of the lines we just entered.

Verbosity, synonyms, and "me"

The English-like nature of the programming language in LiveCode is amazingly powerful, but rigidly so. In some other tools, you have a choice of whether you want to use verbose English-like syntax, less verbose, or what is called *dot syntax*. The *Lingo language*, in Adobe Director, is a good comparison.

Suppose we want to change the text inside a field, that is the first entry of a director movie's cast, we can perform the following verbose syntax:

```
put "hello world" into the text of member 1
```

We can perform a slightly less verbose syntax:

```
the text of member 1 = "hello world"
```

Or, we can perform a dot-syntax:

```
member(1).text = "hello world"
```

In LiveCode, there isn't a choice. What you type has to be in the form of:

```
put value into container
```

However, you do have a choice about whether to use a long version of a word, short version, or an abbreviated form. There are also synonyms, which allow you to use a word that makes more sense to you.

Here are the two ways of saying the same thing, with the second variation using an abbreviated form of the keywords:

```
put character 3 of word 2 of card field "name of field 1" into
aVariable
put char 3 of word 2 of fld 1 into aVariable
```

When you are dealing with the contents of the object that has the script running, you can use the keyword me to save on some typing, and LiveCode will also try to work out what you have in mind, if possible.

Take the lines we have entered as examples:

```
numberPressed the label of me
```

Here, `numberPressed` will propagate up to a card handler that we will add (soon) and `the label of me` will look at the Label that you have set for the object that the script is inside of:

```
set the clipboarddata["TEXT"] to me
```

In this case, `me` would normally refer to the object (as is the case with `the label of me`), but because we gave the extra clue of `["TEXT"]`, LiveCode knows that it's the text contents of the field that have the script and not the field itself. Still, because there is potential for confusion, when reading your own code later, you could add a couple of words to make the meaning more clear:

```
set the clipboarddata["TEXT"] to the text of me
```

> By the way, the display field script is not needed for the calculator to work. It's just there so that at any point of time, you can click on the field and have the current value copied to the clipboard in order to paste it in other applications.

You might choose to be more verbose than is needed, just for readability reasons, and in these chapters, this is going to be the case. It is easier to tell what is going to happen by using:

```
put the text of me into textvariable
```

The following will be less verbose compared to the preceding entry, even though they are equally valid:

```
put me into textVariable
```

In either case, as it's a field, LiveCode knows what you meant.

You see in the script that we typed `short name of me`, what's that all about? Objects in LiveCode have a lengthy description of where they are located, for example, the `buttonname` button of the `1234` card ID of the `path/to/stack.livecode` stack. In the calculator application, we need only the single word that you set as the name of the button. If we asked for `name of me`, it would still say "the `buttonname` button". To just grab the name itself, we use `short name of me`.

There are times when you will want to use the other variations of name, including the long name and the abbreviated name, which you can read about in the LiveCode Dictionary entry for name. In addition to a description of the different ways to use name, there are a number of cautions you need to be aware of.

Case sensitivity

If any of you use advanced LiveCode, you may notice that in some cases, I have the casing wrong. LiveCode doesn't mind what casing you have used and so, when I incorrectly said clipboarddata instead of clipboardData, it didn't matter. This feature isn't unique to LiveCode, but it is common among near-English programming languages to not demand that the user gets the casing exactly right before the command works.

Adding the card handlers

If you dared to go ahead and tried using the calculator buttons, you will see a lot of script errors. We need to add in the card level handlers to be at the receiving end of the calls that the buttons make. Instead of walking you through, typing a line of code at a time, it probably would be quicker to present the lines in one go and explain what each line does. As a practice run, here are the lines that we have entered so far:

On all the number buttons and the decimal point button, you should have this script:

```
on mouseup
  numberPressed the label of me
end mouseup
```

The on mouseUp event is triggered when you press and release the left mouse button while on the numberPressed call. This event will call a card handler named numberPressed, passing with it, the label that you had set for the button that holds this script.

The **C** (clear) button has this script:

```
on mouseUp
  clearPressed
end mouseUp
```

The clearPressed event will call a card script named clearPressed.

The other buttons all work the same way; they call a handler of the name used, which we're about to add to the card script. This is script for the **+**, **-**, *****, and **/** buttons, passing to the card level, the name of the button in question:

```
on mouseUp
  operatorPressed the short name of me
end mouseUp
```

The following script is for the +- button:

```
on mouseUp
   toggleSign
end mouseUp
```

The display field has this script:

```
on mouseUp
   set the clipboardData ["TEXT"] to me
end mouseUp
```

In the field's case, only one line of code is being executed, so no need to put that up on the card level, unless we had a lot of fields doing the same thing.

So, why don't we add all those card level scripts! We will take them one at a time, with an explanation of how each one works. But first, let's see how LiveCode handles variables.

Downloading the example code

You can download the example code files for all Packt books you have purchased from your account at `http://www.packtpub.com`. If you purchased this book elsewhere, you can visit `http://www.packtpub.com/support` and register to have the files e-mailed directly to you.

Variable types in LiveCode

Generally speaking, variables are memory locations where you store values that you need to access later, but in most programming languages, you can dictate which routines have access to which variables. Less English-like languages may include the terms `public`, `private`, and `protected`. Things are not that different in LiveCode, but words are used that more accurately describe the region that the variable can be used in. If a variable is to be readable everywhere, it would be `global`. If it's just to be used in the current script, it's `local`.

LiveCode also has custom property variables, and as an aside, many people would use these for performing the calculator button values instead of relying on the label of the button. Perhaps, we'll use them later!

Now, where was I... oh yes, card level scripts. This is the first line of the card script:

```
global currentTotal, currentValue, currentCommand, newNumber
```

As discussed, these are the variables that will allow the many handlers to pass values to each other. In this case, the variables could be local, but often, you may make them global instead, thinking that a case may come up later where you need to get at the variables from outside the script you're in.

It's good to reset things when you start the app and LiveCode has an openCard event that we can pick up on. The following code resets things:

```
on openCard
  clearPressed
end openCard

on clearPressed
  put true into newNumber
  put 0 into field "display"
  put 0 into currentTotal
  put 0 into currentValue
  put empty into currentCommand
end clearPressed
```

Having the reset lines in their own clearPressed handler will allow us to call it at other times, not just when the card opens, and we do call it directly when we click on the **C** clear button. This will zero out the display field, the running total for your calculation and the last number that you entered into the calculator. It also clears the variable that is used to remember which operator button you last pressed, and a Boolean (true or false) variable is used to recognize whether a number button that you press should clear the display or append to the display.

All the numbered buttons and the decimal point button call this handler:

```
on numberPressed n
  if newnumber is true then
    put n into field "display"
    put false into newnumber
  else
    put n after field "display"
  end if
end numberPressed
```

The n comment after the handler name, is a parameter variable that stores the content that was sent to the handler. In this case, it's the label of the button that was pressed. All this routine needs to add is a character to the end of the display field, except when you are typing in a new number. That's where the newNumber Boolean variable comes in; if it is set to true, the incoming character replaces all the contents of the display field. If it's false, the character is added to the end of the field.

This is the handler to be used when you press the **+**, **-**, *****, or **/**, buttons:

```
on operatorPressed operator
  if currentCommand is empty then
    put field "display" into currentTotal
    put operator into currentCommand
    put true into newNumber
  else
    put operator into currentCommand
    equalsPressed
  end if
end operatorPressed
```

When you use a calculator, you type in one number, an operator, and then another number, followed by either another operator or the `equals` button. Now you press the operator button as there is no way to know what you're doing (since you haven't entered the next number in the calculation yet), so we have to remember the operator when we press the equals button. If the `currentCommand` variable doesn't already have a value, we store the display field text into a `currentTotal` variable, store the operator character that you pressed into the `currentCommand` variable, and make sure that `newNumber` is set to `true`. Doing this makes sure that the next number button you press will clear the display field. If `currentCommand` already has a value, we replace it with the new value and then call the same handler that is used when you press the `equals` button.

There are most likely shorter ways to cope with the `equals` button being pressed, but here, we'll use several `if` statements and run the appropriate calculation code:

```
on equalsPressed
  put field "display" into currentValue
  if currentCommand is empty then exit equalsPressed
  if currentCommand is "divide" then put currentTotal /
    currentValue into field "display"
  if currentCommand is "multiply" then put currentTotal *
    currentValue into field "display"
  if currentCommand is "minus" then put currentTotal -
    currentValue into field "display"
  if currentCommand is "plus" then put currentTotal +
    currentValue into field "display"
  put field "display" into currentTotal
  put true into newNumber
  put empty into currentCommand
end equalsPressed
```

The contents of the display field are stored in the `currentValue` variable and the last operator button you pressed (that is stored in `currentCommand`) is looked at, to see what happens next. If there wasn't a previous operator, as would be the case if you pressed "equals" twice in a row, we'd ignore the button press and exit the routine. For the four operators, we do the appropriate calculation. Afterwards, we store the new running total in the `currentTotal` variable, make sure that the `newNumber` Boolean is `true` (so that the next number button pressed will clear the display field), and we forget the last operator button that was pressed by putting `empty` in the `currentCommand` variable.

One thing to note is that LiveCode is smart enough to know that the text string inside the display field is to be treated as a floating-point number.

The `togglesign` last handler is as follows:

```
on togglesign
  if character 1 of field "display" is "-" then
    delete character 1 of field "display"
  else
    put "-" before field "display"
  end if
end togglesign
```

This is a very simple routine that doesn't have to understand that it's floating point numbers are being represented. It simply checks whether the first character is a minus or not and if it is, it deletes the character; if not, it inserts a hyphen that LiveCode will later interpret as a negative value.

Pop quiz – try to remember...

As you get to learn a new tool, you can end up taking a lot of time remembering where everything you may need, is located. You know what you want to do, you know how to do it, but you can't remember where that thing is located! For example:

Q1. Where did you go to set the text styling for the calculator's title field?

1. The **Edit** menu.
2. The **Object** menu.
3. The **Text Formatting** section of the **Inspector** palette.
4. The **Text** menu.

Answer: 3

Getting to this section involved selecting the Edit tool from the Tools palette, clicking on the title field on card 1, and choosing **Text Formatting** from the Inspector palette drop-down menu. However, there is indeed a Text menu. Really, that's what we should have used!

Extending the calculator

It is possible to add more features to the simple calculator. If we consider the functions in the card script and how the buttons are named, we can start to see the processes that are involved in adding a new ability, some of these processes are as follows:

- The calculator operator buttons are named so that the card script knows which one you clicked on.

- When the "equals" button is pressed there is a set of `if` statements in the `equalsPressed` handler that determine what happens next.

Have a go hero – getting to the root of things

On Windows, you can add a square root symbol with `Alt 251` and on Mac, with the shortcut *option + v*. Unfortunately, LiveCode doesn't like these as button labels! At least on Mac, when you type the character in the Inspector palette, the character immediately vanishes. One workaround would be to use the message box and type this:

```
set the label of btn "squareroot" to "√"
```

This should give you the right symbol as the button label.

LiveCode has a square root function; typing this in the Message Box would produce the square root of 10:

```
put sqrt(10)
```

Now that you are armed with the given information, try to add a square root feature to the calculator.

Other interface controls

So far, we only needed to look at the buttons and fields to be able to create the calculator. In the later chapters, we will use many more controls, so let's take a sneak peek at those.

The video player control

LiveCode can play movies using the Player control type. These can be added to the card in several ways and then using a script command:

- A file can be added from your hard drive by selecting **Import as Control/Video File...** from the **File** menu

- An empty player can be created by selecting **New Control/Player** from the **Object** menu

- A player control can be dragged from the **Tools** palette to the card. In this case, a sample movie is included

- A player along with its name can be created with the code:

```
new player "player name"
```

Having added the player to the card, you can then set the video file to be played by entering the file path or URL of the file under the **Basic Settings** option of the **Inspector** palette. You can also set the path to the video with script:

```
set the filename of player "player name" to "file path or URL"
```

The still image control

In much the same way as you just saw for the playing of video, still images can be added to a stack. All of the options shown to add a video player can be done in the same way for images. Here, for example, is the script needed to add the RunRev company logo to the card:

```
new image "revlogo"
set the filename of image "revlogo" to "http://runrev.com/wp-content/
themes/runrev2013/ims/runrev_logo.png"
```

Rollover buttons

Images that you import can be used as icons in a button. To set up a button, so that it has a nice idle state image and an associated highlight image, you would have to go through the following steps:

1. Select **File | Import As Control | Image File...**.

2. Choose the images that represent the idle and highlight states and click on **Open**.

3. Select the button that you wish to look like these images, and under **Icons & Border** in the **Inspector** palette, click on the magic wand button to the right of the top entry ("Icon").

4. In the dialog that appears, select **This Stack** from the drop-down menu.

5. Select the image that is in the idle state for the button.

6. Click on the magic wand button next to the **Hilite** entry and choose the highlight state image.

7. Under **Basic Properties**, choose the transparent button from the Style drop-down menu.

8. Uncheck the boxes for **Show name**, **Auto hilite**, and **Shared hilite**.

9. Resize the button to be big enough to show the image.

10. Select each of the original images, and under **Basic Properties**, uncheck the **Visible box**.

In the following screenshot, we can see two images that have been imported in order to give the **Begin** button a more iOS-like appearance. The button is selected and the **Inspector** palette shows the icon selection choices:

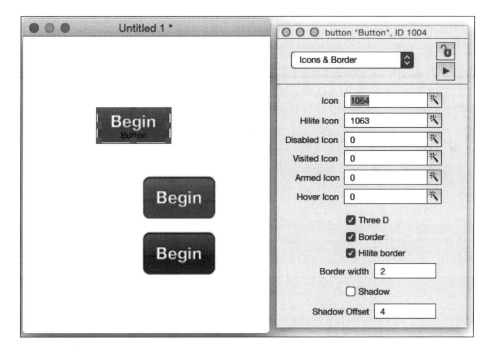

When you choose an image for use, the button itself is updated. In this case, the **Hilite** icon has been set to the darker version of the graphic, but as shown here, the button still needs to be resized.

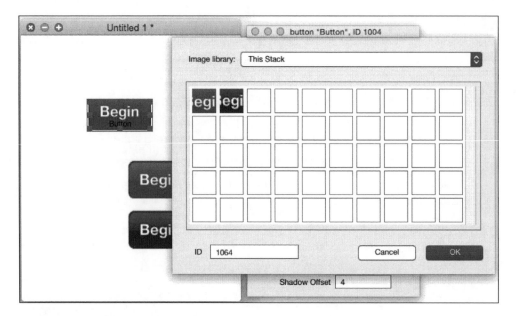

Many more controls...

LiveCode has a lot of different controls. Many are just slight variations, but there are plenty that are quite different from each other. Look at the **Object** menu and **New Control**. As you'll see, the list is very long!

Debugging

If you went ahead and tried out the calculator before we entered all the scripts it needed, you most likely will have seen the script debugging in action. Hopefully, you've managed to cope with what you saw, it can be overwhelming at first. This is what it would have looked like:

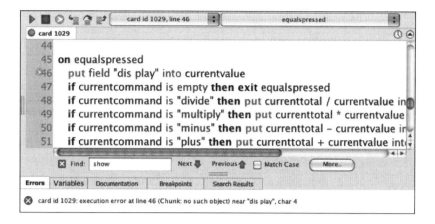

Most of what you see here is the same that you'll see when you edit scripts, but if you do see the debug variation, you are actually in a paused state, which is a freeze frame of the program as it runs. In this example, the program stopped because line 46 is looking for a field named `dis play`. There isn't such a field, as it should be `display`.

The error message at the bottom of the panel makes it clear that the error has something to do with the field name and you can quickly spot the typo. Sometimes though, you may need to inspect the variables to make sure they contain the values you think they should, for example, the **Variables** tab will show a list of those values.

An unexpected problem is one time that you may see the debugger, but when developing a script, you are able to set breakpoints by clicking in the column just to the left of the line number you want to halt the program at.

Once the script is halted by a breakpoint, you can use the row of buttons at the top to step through the code. The content displayed as you hover the cursor above a button, is it's meaning. These buttons are:

- ◆ **Continue**: This will set the script that runs again
- ◆ **Stop**: This stops the script from running and switches to the editor, so that you can make changes
- ◆ **Show next statement**: This will show an indicator to the left of the current line
- ◆ **Step into next statement**: This is used for stepping into a different handler
- ◆ **Step over next statement**: This is used to go onto the next statement in the current handler without stepping in a handler mentioned on the current line
- ◆ **Step out of current handler**: This is used to skip the remaining lines in a handler that you had previously stepped into and to exit to the handler that called the current one

You will become familiar with the script editor and debugger as you go along, but that should get you started!

In this chapter, we covered just enough to make you familiar with the environment so that you can practice using some controls and to do a little script writing. There is quite a lot to LiveCode as a tool, so you may be interested to look into other topics or go into more depth than is covered here.

A good starting point would be LiveCode's own set of online tutorials, which are located at `http://lessons.runrev.com/`.

Type in the search box, words that describe your area of interest and you will see a list of articles on that topic.

Summary

Having created a simple calculator from scratch, you should by now be more familiar with the LiveCode environment.

In this chapter, we covered buttons, fields, scripts, and the stack structure to get an understanding of how they work together. We also showed several short scripts to illustrate the English-like syntax used by LiveCode while using the script window to debug a script.

We then examined other interface controls in preparation to use those in later chapters of this book.

We also discussed the kinds of variables used by LiveCode and how it can use abbreviated commands and synonyms.

Now that you've learned enough to make regular LiveCode stacks, we need to download and install additional software from Google and Apple that is required to publish a stack to a mobile device and then we need to begin trying out mobile-specific features—both of which are covered in the next chapter.

2

Getting Started with LiveCode Mobile

Before we can do neat things...

Creating stacks that do something useful or eventually become a mobile app that you can sell is a very gratifying process. Minute by minute, you can make progress and instantly see the improvements you have made. Unfortunately, there is a lot of less gratifying work to be done before and after you make your masterpiece. This chapter will take you through the "before" part.

LiveCode makes mobile apps by taking the stack you have made along with any supporting files you have added, and compiles the application file using the developer kit that you download from the mobile OS provider, Google for Android and Apple for iOS.

In this chapter, we will:

- ◆ Sign up for Google Play
- ◆ Sign up for Amazon Appstore
- ◆ Download and install the Android SDK
- ◆ Configure LiveCode so that it knows where to look for the Android SDK
- ◆ Become an iOS developer with Apple
- ◆ Download and install Xcode
- ◆ Configure LiveCode so that it knows where to look for iOS SDKs
- ◆ Set up simulators and physical devices
- ◆ Test a stack in a simulator and physical device

Disclaimer

This chapter references many Internet pages that are not under our control. Here, we do show screenshots or URLs, so remember that the content may have changed since we wrote this. The suppliers may also have changed some of the details, but in general, our description of procedures should still work the way we have described them.

Here we go...

iOS, Android, or both?

It could be that you only have interest in iOS or Android. You should be able to easily skip to the sections you're interested in unless you're intrigued about how the other half works! If, like me, you're a capitalist, then you should be interested in both the operating systems.

Far fewer steps are needed to get the Android SDK than the iOS developer tools because for iOS, we have to sign up as a developer with Apple. However, the configuration for Android is more involved. We'll go through all the steps for Android and then the ones for iOS. If you're an iOS-only kind of person, skip the next few pages and start up again at the *Becoming an iOS Developer* section.

Becoming an Android developer

It is possible to develop Android OS apps without signing up for anything. We'll try to be optimistic and assume that within the next 12 months, you will find time to make an awesome app that will make you rich! To that end, we'll go over everything that is involved in the process of signing up to publish your apps in both Google Play (formally known as Android Market) and Amazon Appstore.

Google Play

The starting location to open Google Play is `http://developer.android.com/`:

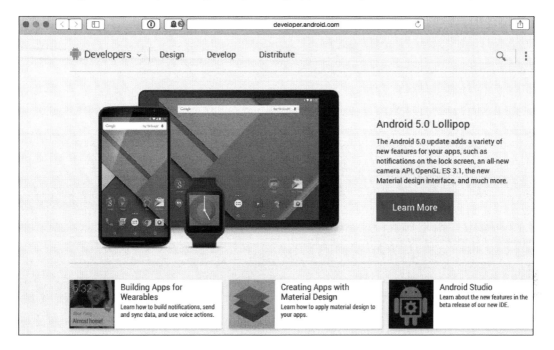

We will come back to this page again, shortly to download the Android SDK, but for now, click on the **Distribute** link in the menu bar and then on the **Developer Console** button on the following screen. Since Google changes these pages occasionally, you can use the URL `https://play.google.com/apps/publish/` or search for "Google Play Developer Console". The screens you will progress through are not shown here since they tend to change with time.

There will be a sign-in page; sign in using your usual Google details.

Which e-mail address to use?

Some Google services are easier to sign up for if you have a Gmail account. Creating a Google+ account, or signing up for some of their cloud services, requires a Gmail address (or so it seemed to me at the time!). If you have previously set up Google Wallet as part of your account, some of the steps in signing up become simpler. So, use your Gmail address and if you don't have one, create one!

Google charges you a $25 fee to sign up for Google Play. At least now, you know about this! Enter the developer name, e-mail address, website URL (if you have one), and your phone number. The payment of $25 will be done through Google Wallet, which will save you from entering the billing details yet again.

Now, you're all signed up and ready to make your fortune!

Amazon Appstore

Although the rules and costs for Google Play are fairly relaxed, Amazon has a more Apple-like approach, both in the amount they charge you to register and in the review process to accept app submissions. The URL to open Amazon Appstore is `http://developer.amazon.com/public`:

Follow these steps to start with Amazon Appstore:

1. When you select **Get Started**, you need to sign in to your Amazon account.

> **Which email address to use?**
>
> This feels like déjà vu! There is no real advantage of using your Google e-mail address when signing up for the Amazon Appstore Developer Program, but if you happen to have an account with Amazon, sign in with that one. It will simplify the payment stage, and your developer account and the general Amazon account will be associated with each other.

2. You are then asked to agree to the Appstore Distribution Agreement terms before learning about the costs.

3. These costs are $99 per year, but the first year is free. So that's good!

4. Unlike the Google Android Market, Amazon asks for your bank details up front, ready to send you lots of money later, we hope!

5. That's it, you're ready to make another fortune to go along with the one that Google sent you!

Pop quiz – when is something too much?

You're at the end of developing your mega app, it's 49.5 MB in size, and you just need to add title screen music. Why would you not add the two-minute epic tune you have lined up?

1. It would take too long to load.

2. People tend to skip the title screen soon anyway.

3. The file size is going to be over 50 MB.

4. Heavy metal might not be appropriate for a children's storybook app!

Answer: 3

The other answers are valid too, though you could play the music as an external sound to reduce loading time, but if your file size goes over 50 MB, you would then cut out potential sales from people who are connected by cellular and not wireless networks. At the time of writing this book, all the stores require that you be connected to the site via a wireless network if you intend to download apps that are over 50 MB.

Downloading the Android SDK

Head back to `http://developer.android.com/` and click on the **Get the SDK** link or go straight to `http://developer.android.com/sdk/index.html`. This link defaults to the OS that you are running on. Click on the **Other Download Options** link to see the full set of options for other systems, as shown here:

^ VIEW ALL DOWNLOADS AND SIZES

ADT Bundle

Platform	Package	Size	MD5 Checksum
Windows 32-bit	adt-bundle-windows-x86-20140702.zip	370612741 bytes	9d2cf3770edbb49461788164af2331f3
Windows 64-bit	adt-bundle-windows-x86_64-20140702.zip	370763706 bytes	bfc3472a12173422ba044182ac466c13
Mac OS X 64-bit	adt-bundle-mac-x86_64-20140702.zip	320593642 bytes	24c51a1ad96c5f6d43821d978bf9866d
Linux 32-bit	adt-bundle-linux-x86-20140702.zip	371950735 bytes	5901c898bae4fe95476463a951b68404
Linux 64-bit	adt-bundle-linux-x86_64-20140702.zip	372259418 bytes	18a7c5778f96c0823349d465f58a0a36

SDK Tools Only

Platform	Package	Size	MD5 Checksum
Windows 32 & 64-bit	android-sdk_r23.0.2-windows.zip	141435413 bytes	89f0576abf3f362a700767bdc2735c8a
	installer_r23.0.2-windows.exe (Recommended)	93015376 bytes	7be4b9c230341e1fb57c0f84a8df3994
Mac OS X 32 & 64-bit	android-sdk_r23.0.2-macosx.zip	90996733 bytes	322787b0e6c629d926c28690c79ac0d8
Linux 32 & 64-bit	android-sdk_r23.0.2-linux.tgz	140827643 bytes	94a8c62086a7398cc0e73e1c8e65f71e

> In this book, we're only going to cover Windows and Mac OS X (Intel) and only as much as is needed to make LiveCode work with the Android and iOS SDKs. If you intend to make native Java-based applications, you may be interested in reading through all the steps that are described in the web page `http://developer.android.com/sdk/installing.html`.

Click on the SDK download link for your platform. Note that you don't need the ADT Bundle unless you plan to develop outside the LiveCode IDE. The steps you'll have to go through are different for Mac and Windows. Let's start with Mac.

Installing the Android SDK on Mac OS X (Intel)

LiveCode itself doesn't require Intel Mac; you can develop stacks using a PowerPC-based Mac, but both the Android SDK and some of the iOS tools require an Intel-based Mac, which sadly means that if you're reading this as you sit next to your Mac G4 or G5, you're not going to get too far!

The Android SDK requires the **Java Runtime Environment** (JRE). Since Apple stopped including the JRE in more recent OS X systems, you should check whether you have it in your system by typing `java -version` in a Terminal window. The terminal will display the version of Java installed. If not, you may get a message like the following:

Click on the **More Info** button and follow the instructions to install the JRE and verify its installation. At the time of writing this book, JRE 8 doesn't work with OS X 10.10 and I had to use the JRE 6 obtained from `http://support.apple.com/kb/DL1572`.

The file that you just downloaded will automatically expand to show a folder named `android-sdk-macosx`. It may be in your `downloads` folder right now, but a more natural place for it would be in your `Documents` folder, so move it there before performing the next steps.

There is an SDK readme text file that lists the steps you need to follow during the installation. If these steps are different to what we have here, then follow the steps in the readme file in case they have been updated since the procedure here was written.

Open the **Terminal** application, which is in **Applications/Utilities**. You need to change the default directories present in the `android-sdk-macosx` folder. One handy trick, using Terminal, is that you can drag items into the Terminal window to get the file path to that item. Using this trick, you can type `cd` and a space in the Terminal window and then drag the `android-sdk-macosx` folder after the space character. You'll end up with this line if your username is Fred:

```
new-host-3:~ fred$ cd /Users/fred/Documents/android-sdk-macosx
```

Of course, the first part of the line and the user folder will match yours, not Fred's!

Whatever your name is, press the *Return* or *Enter* key after entering the preceding line. The location line now changes to look like this:

```
new-host-3:android-sdk-macosx colin$
```

Either carefully type or copy and paste the following line from the readme file:

```
tools/android update sdk --no-ui
```

Press *Return* or *Enter* again. How long the file takes to get downloaded depends on your Internet connection. Even with a very fast Internet connection, it could still take over an hour.

If you care to follow the update progress, you can just run the `android` file in the `tools` directory. This will open the Android SDK Manager, which is similar to the Windows version shown a couple of pages further on in this book.

Installing the Android SDK on Windows

The downloads page recommends that you use the `.exe` download link, as it gives extra services to you, such as checking whether you have the **Java Development Kit** (**JDK**) installed. When you click on the link, either use the **Run** or **Save** options, as you would with any download of a Windows installer. Here, we've opted to use **Run**; if you use **Save**, then you need to open the file after it has been saved to your hard drive. In the following case, as the JDK wasn't installed, a dialog box appears saying go to Oracle's site to get the JDK:

If you see this screen too, you can leave the dialog box open and click on the **Visit java.oracle. com** button. On the Oracle page, click on a checkbox to agree to their terms and then on the download link that corresponds with your platform. Choose the 64-bit option if you are running a 64-bit version of Windows or the x86 option if you are running a 32-bit version of Windows.

Either way, you're greeted with another installer that you can Run or Save as you prefer. Naturally, it takes a while for the installer to do its thing too! When the installation is complete, you will see a JDK registration page and it's up to you, to register or not.

Back at the Android SDK installer dialog box, you can click on the **Back** button and then the **Next** button to get back to the JDK checking stage; only now, it sees that you have the JDK installed. Complete the remaining steps of the SDK installer as you would with any Windows installer.

One important thing to note is that the last screen of the installer offers to open the SDK Manager. You should do that, so resist the temptation to uncheck that box!

Click on Finish and you'll be greeted with a command-line window for a few moments, as shown in the following screenshot, and then, the Android SDK Manager will appear and do its thing:

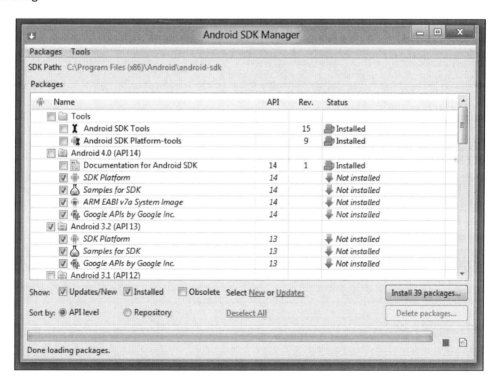

As with the Mac version, it takes a very long time for all these add-ons to download.

Pointing LiveCode to the Android SDK

After all the installation and command-line work, it's a refreshing change to get back to LiveCode!

Open the **LiveCode Preferences** and choose **Mobile Support**:

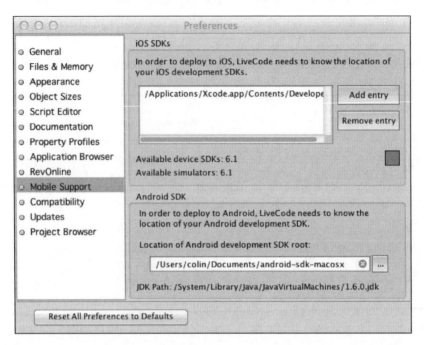

We will set the two iOS entries after we get iOS going (but these options will be grayed out in Windows). For now, click on the **...** button next to the Android development SDK root field and navigate to where the SDK is installed. If you've followed the earlier steps correctly, then the SDK will be in the `Documents` folder on Mac or you can navigate to `C:\Program Files (x86)\Android\` to find it on Windows (or somewhere else, if you choose to use a custom location).

Depending on the APIs that were loaded in the SDK Manager, you may get a message that the path does not include support for Android 2.2 (API 8). If so, use the Android SDK Manager to install it. LiveCode seems to want API 8 even though at this time Android 5.0 uses API 21.

Phew! Now, let's do the same for iOS...

Pop quiz – tasty code names

An Android OS uses some curious code names for each version. At the time of writing this book, we were on Android OS 5, which had a code name of Lollipop. Version 4.1 was Jelly Bean and version 4.4 was KitKat. Which of these is most likely to be the code name for the next Android OS?

1. Lemon Cheesecake

2. Munchies

3. Noodle

4. Marshmallow

Answer: 4

The pattern, if it isn't obvious, is that the code name takes on the next letter of the alphabet, is a kind of food, but more specifically, it's a dessert. "Munchies" almost works for Android OS 6, but "Marshmallow" or "Meringue Pie" would be a better choices!

Becoming an iOS developer

Creating iOS LiveCode applications requires that LiveCode must have access to the iOS SDK. This is installed as part of the Xcode developer tools and is a Mac-only program. Also, when you upload an app to the iOS App Store, the application used is Mac only and is part of the Xcode installation. If you are a Windows-based developer and wish to develop and publish for iOS, you need either an actual Mac based system or a virtual machine that can run the Mac OS. We can even use VirtualBox for running a Mac based virtual machine, but performance will be an issue. Refer to `http://apple.stackexchange.com/questions/63147/is-mac-os-x-in-a-virtualbox-vm-suitable-for-ios-development` for more information.

The biggest difference between becoming an Android developer and becoming an iOS developer is that you have to sign up with Apple for their developer program even if you never produce an app for the iOS App Store, but no such signing up is required when becoming an Android developer. If things go well and you end up making an app for various stores, then this isn't such a big deal. It will cost you $25 to submit an app to the Android Market, $99 a year (with the first year free) to submit an app to the Amazon Appstore, and $99 a year (including the first year) to be an iOS developer with Apple. Just try to sell more than 300 copies of your amazing $0.99 app and you'll find that it has paid for itself!

Note that there is a free iOS App Store and app licensing included, with LiveCode Membership, which also costs $99 per year. As a LiveCode member, you can submit your free non-commercial app to RunRev who will provide a license that will allow you to submit your app as "closed source" to iOS App Store. This service is exclusively available for LiveCode members. The first submission each year is free; after that, there is a $25 administration fee per submission. Refer to `http://livecode.com/membership/` for more information.

You can enroll yourself in the iOS Developer Program for iOS at `http://developer.apple.com/programs/ios/`:

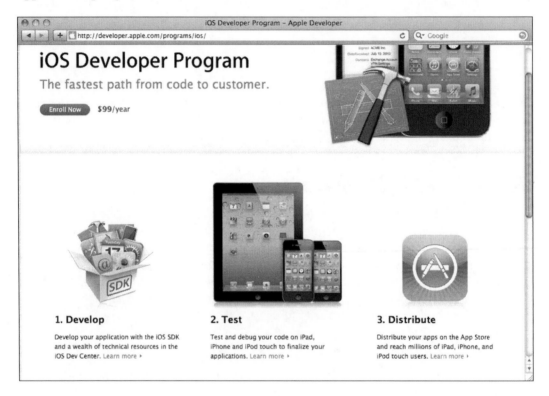

While signing up to be an iOS developer, there are a number of possibilities when it comes to your current status. If you already have an Apple ID, which you use with your iTunes or Apple online store purchases, you could choose the **I already have an Apple ID...** option. In order to illustrate all the steps to sign up, we will start as a brand new user, as shown in the following screenshot:

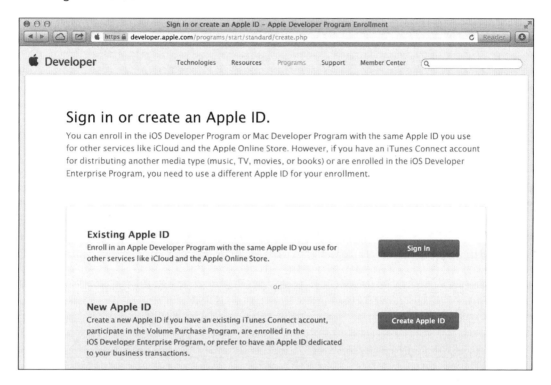

You can choose whether you want to sign up as an individual or as a company. We will choose **Individual**, as shown in the following screenshot:

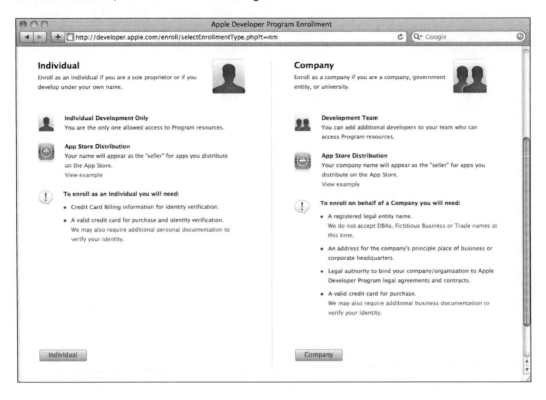

With any such sign up process, you need to enter your personal details, set a security question, and enter your postal address:

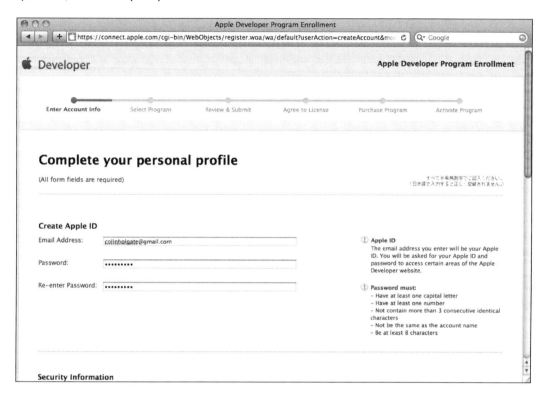

Most Apple software and services have their own legal agreement for you to sign. The one shown in the following screenshot is the general **Registered Apple Developer Agreement**:

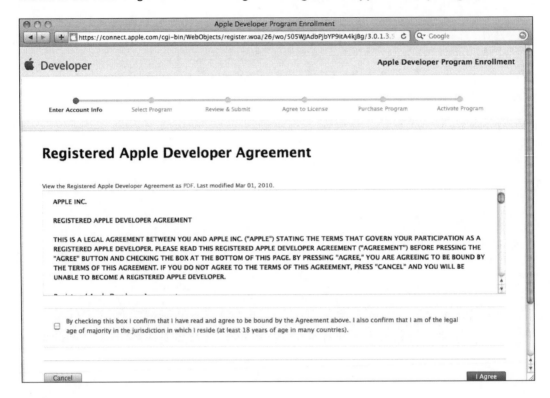

In order to verify the e-mail address you have used, a verification code is sent to you with a link in the e-mail, you can click this, or enter the code manually. Once you have completed the verification code step, you can then enter your billing details.

It could be that you might go on to make LiveCode applications for the Mac App Store, in which case, you will need to add the **Mac Developer Program** product. For our purpose, we only need to sign up for the iOS Developer Program, as shown in the following screenshot:

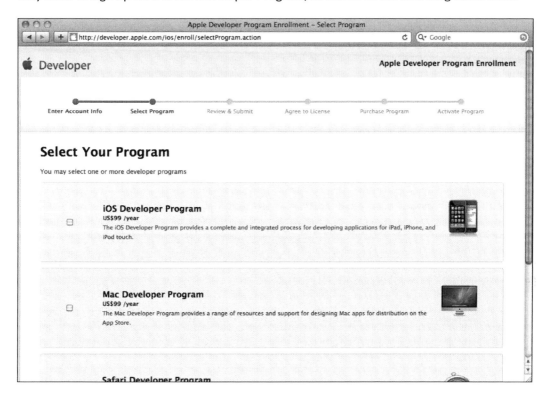

Each product that you sign up for has its own agreement. Lots of small print to read!

The actual purchasing of the iOS developer account is handled through the Apple Store of your own region, shown as follows:

As you can see in the next screenshot, it is going to cost you $99 per year or $198 per year if you also sign up for the Mac Developer account. Most LiveCode users won't need to sign up for the Mac Developer account unless their plan is to submit desktop apps to the Mac App Store.

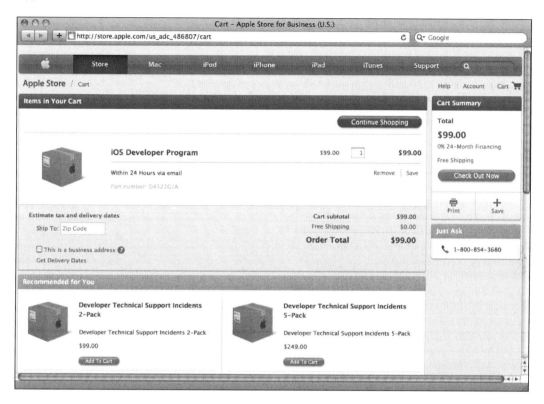

After submitting the order, you are rewarded with a message that tells you that you are now registered as an Apple developer!

Sadly, you won't get an instant approval, as was the case with Android Market or Amazon Appstore. You have to wait for the approval for five days. In the early iPhone Developer days, the approval could take a month or more, so 24 hours is an improvement!

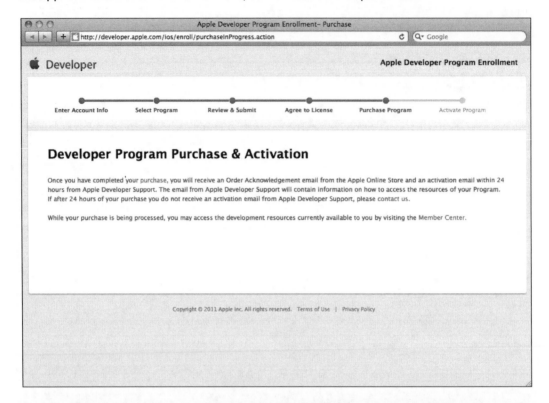

Pop quiz – iOS code names

You had it easy with the pop quiz about Android OS code names! Not so with iOS.

Which of these names is more likely to be a code name for a future version of iOS?

1. Las Vegas
2. Laguna Beach
3. Hunter Mountain
4. Death Valley

Answer: 3

Although not publicized, Apple does use code names for each version of iOS. Previous examples included Big Bear, Apex, Kirkwood, and Telluride. These, and all the others are apparently ski resorts. Hunter Mountain is a relatively small mountain (3,200 feet), so if it does get used, perhaps it would be a minor update!

Installing Xcode

Once you receive confirmation of becoming an iOS developer, you will be able to log in to the iOS Dev Center at `https://developer.apple.com/devcenter/ios/index.action`.

This same page is used by iOS developers who are not using LiveCode and is full of support documents that can help you create native applications using Xcode and Objective-C. We don't need all the support documents, but we do need to download Xcode's support documents.

In the downloads area of the iOS Dev Center page, you will see a link to the current version of Xcode and a link to get to the older versions as well. The current version is delivered via Mac App Store; when you try the given link, you will see a button that takes you to the App Store application.

Installing Xcode from Mac App Store is very straightforward. It's just like buying any other app from the store, except that it's free! It does require you to use the latest version of Mac OS X. Xcode will show up in your `Applications` folder.

If you are using an older system, then you need to download one of the older versions from the developer page. The older Xcode installation process is much like the installation process of any other Mac application:

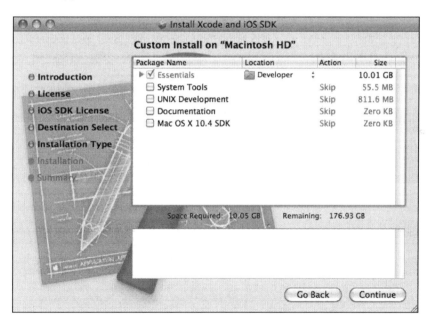

The older version of Xcode takes a long time to get installed, but in the end, you should have the `Developer` folder or a new Xcode application ready for LiveCode.

Coping with newer and older devices

In early 2012, Apple brought to the market a new version of iPad. The main selling point of this one compared to iPad 2 is that it has a Retina display. The original iPads have a resolution of 1024 x 768 and the Retina version has a resolution of 2048 x 1536. If you wish to build applications to take advantage of this, you must get the current version of Xcode from Mac App Store and not one of the older versions from the developer page. The new version of Xcode demands that you work on Mac OS 10.10 or its later versions. So, to fully support the latest devices, you may have to update your system software more than you were expecting! But wait, there's more... By taking a later version of Xcode, you are missing the iOS SDK versions needed to support older iOS devices, such as the original iPhone and iPhone 3G. Fortunately, you can go to Preferences in Xcode where there is a Downloads tab where you can get these older SDKs downloaded in the new version of Xcode. Typically, Apple only allows you to download one version older than the one that is currently provided in Xcode. There are older versions available, but are not accepted by Apple for App Store submission.

Pointing LiveCode to the iOS SDKs

Open the LiveCode **Preferences** and choose **Mobile Support**:

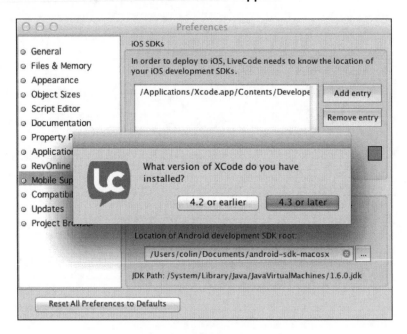

Click on the **Add Entry** button in the upper-right section of the window to see a dialog box that asks whether you are using Xcode 4.2 or 4.3 or a later version. If you choose 4.2, then go on to select the folder named `Developer` at the root of your hard drive. For 4.3 or later versions, choose the Xcode application itself in your `Applications` folder. LiveCode knows where to find the SDKs for iOS.

Before we make our first mobile app...

Now that the required SDKs are installed and LiveCode knows where they are, we can make a stack and test it in a simulator or on a physical device. We do, however, have to get the simulators and physical devices warmed up...

Getting ready for test development on an Android device

Simulating on iOS is easier than it is on Android, and testing on a physical device is easier on Android than on iOS, but the setting up of physical Android devices can be horrendous!

Time for action – starting an Android Virtual Device

You will have to dig a little deep in the Android SDK folders to find the Android Virtual Device setup program. You might as well provide a shortcut or an alias to it for quicker access. The following steps will help you setup and start an Android virtual device:

1. Navigate to the Android SDK tools folder located at `C:\Program Files (x86)\Android\android-sdk\` on Windows and navigate to your `Documents/android-sdk-macosx/tools` folder on Mac.

2. Open **AVD Manager** on Windows or **android** on Mac (these look like a Unix executable file; just double-click on it and the application will open via a command-line window).

3. If you're on Mac, select **Manage AVDs...** from the **Tools** menu.

4. Select **Tablet** from the list of devices if there is one. If not, you can add your own custom devices as described in the following section.

5. Click on the **Start** button.

6. Sit patiently while the virtual device starts up!

7. Open LiveCode, create a new **Mainstack**, and click on **Save** to save the stack to your hard drive.

8. Navigate to **File | Standalone Application Settings...**.

9. Click on the Android icon and click on the **Build for Android** checkbox to select it.

10. Close the settings dialog box and take a look at the **Development** menu.

11. If the virtual machine is up and running, you should see it listed in the **Test Target** submenu.

Creating an Android Virtual Device

If there are no devices listed when you open the **Android Virtual Device (AVD)** Manager, you may If you wish to create a device, so click on the **Create** button. The following screenshot will appear when you do so. Further explanation of the various fields can be found at `https://developer.android.com/tools/devices/index.html`.

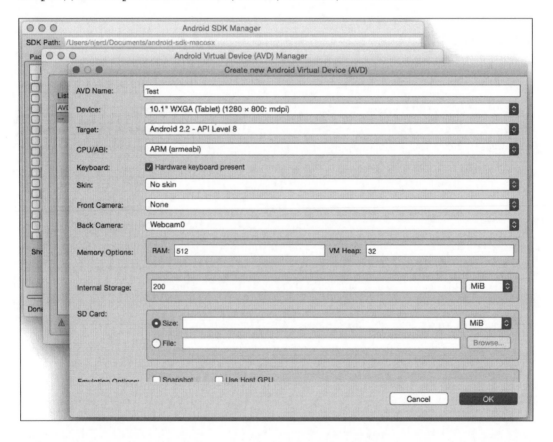

After you have created a device, you can click on **Start** to start the virtual device and change some of the **Launch Options**. You should typically select **Scale display to real size** unless it is too big for your development screen. Then, click on **Launch** to fire up the emulator. Further information on how to run the emulator can be found at `http://developer.android.com/tools/help/emulator.html`.

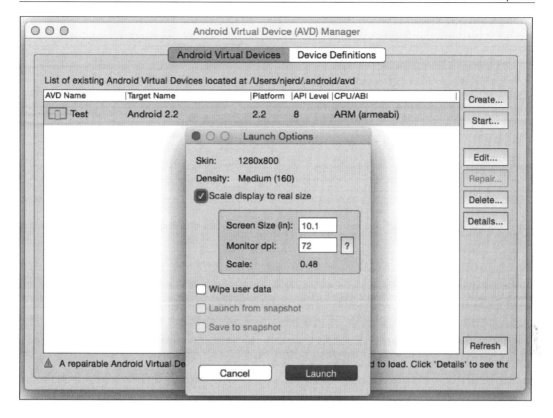

What just happened?

Now that you've opened an Android virtual device, LiveCode will be able to test stacks using this device. Once it has finished loading, that is!

Connecting a physical Android device

Connecting a physical Android device can be extremely straightforward:

1. Connect your device to the system by USB.

2. Select your device from the **Development | Test Target** submenu.

3. Select **Test** from the **Development** menu or click on the **Test** button in the Tool Bar.

There can be problem cases though, and Google Search will become your best friend before you are done solving these problems! We should look at an example problem case, so that you get an idea of how to solve similar situations that you may encounter.

Using Kindle Fire

When it comes to finding Android devices, the Android SDK recognizes a lot of them automatically. Some devices are not recognized and you have to do something to help **Android Debug Bridge (ADB)** find these devices.

Android Debug Bridge (ADB) is part of the Android SDK that acts as an intermediary between your device and any software that needs to access the device. In some cases, you will need to go to the Android system on the device to tell it to allow access for development purposes. For example, on an Android 3 (Honeycomb) device, you need to go to the **Settings | Applications | Development** menu and you need to activate the **USB debugging** mode. Before ADB connects to a Kindle Fire device, that device must first be configured, so that it allows connection. This is enabled by default on the first generation Kindle Fire device. On all other Kindle Fire models, go to the device settings screen, select **Security**, and set **Enable ADB** to **On**.

The original Kindle Fire model comes with USB debugging already enabled, but the ADB system doesn't know about the device at all. You can fix this!

Time for action – adding Kindle Fire to ADB

It only takes one line of text to add Kindle Fire to the list of devices that ADB knows about. The hard part is tracking down the text file to edit and getting ADB to restart after making the required changes. Things are more involved when using Windows than with Mac because you also have to configure the USB driver, so the two systems are shown here as separate steps.

The steps to be followed for adding a Kindle Fire to ADB for a Windows OS are as follows:

1. In Windows Explorer, navigate to `C:\Users\yourusername\.android\` where the `adv_usb.ini` file is located.

2. Open the `adv_usb.ini` text file in a text editor. The file has no visible line breaks, so it is better to use WordPad than NotePad.

3. On the line after the three instruction lines, type `0x1949`.

4. Make sure that there are no blank lines; the last character in the text file would be 9 at the end of `0x1949`.

5. Now, save the file.

6. Navigate to `C:\Program Files (x86)\Android\android-sdk\extras\google\usb_driver\` where `android_winusb.inf` is located.

7. Right-click on the file and in **Properties**, **Security**, select **Users** from the list and click on **Edit** to set the permissions, so that you are allowed to write the file.

8. Open the `android_winusb.inf` file in NotePad.

9. Add the following three lines to the `[Google.NTx86]` and `[Google.NTamd64]` sections and save the file:

```
;Kindle Fire
%SingleAdbInterface% = USB_Install, USB\VID_1949&PID_0006
%CompositeAdbInterface% = USB_Install, USB\VID_1949&PID_0006&MI_01
```

10. You need to set the Kindle so that it uses the Google USB driver that you just edited.

11. In the Windows control panel, navigate to **Device Manager** and find the Kindle entry in the list that is under **USB**.

12. Right-click on the Kindle entry and choose **Update Driver Software…**.

13. Choose the option that lets you find the driver on your local drive, navigate to the `google\usb_driver\` folder, and then select it to be the new driver.

14. When the driver is updated, open a command window (a handy trick to open a command window is to use *Shift*-right-click on the desktop and to choose "Open command window here").

15. Change the directories to where the ADB tool is located by typing:

```
cd C:\Program Files (x86)\Android\android-sdk\platform-tools\
```

16. Type the following three line of code and press Enter after each line:

```
adb kill-server
adb start-server
adb devices
```

17. You should see the Kindle Fire listed (as an obscure looking number) as well as the virtual device if you still have that running.

The steps to be followed for a Mac (MUCH simpler!) system are as follows:

1. Navigate to where the `adv_usb.ini` file is located. On Mac, in Finder, select the menu by navigating to **Go | Go to Folder…** and type `~/.android/`in.

2. Open the `adv_usb.ini` file in a text editor.

3. On the line after the three instruction lines, type `0x1949`.

4. Make sure that there are no blank lines; the last character in the text file would be `9` at the end of `0x1949`.

5. Save the `adv_usb.ini` file.

6. Navigate to **Utilities | Terminal**.

7. You can let OS X know how to find ADB from anywhere by typing the following line (replace `yourusername` with your actual username and also change the path if you've installed the Android SDK to some other location):

```
export PATH=$PATH:/Users/yourusername/Documents/android-sdk-
macosx/platform-tools
```

8. Now, try the same three lines as we did with Windows:

```
adb kill-server
adb start-server
adb devices
```

9. Again, you should see the Kindle Fire listed here.

What just happened?

I suspect that you're going to have nightmares about all these steps! It took a lot of research on the Web to find out some of these obscure hacks. The general case with Android devices on Windows is that you have to modify the USB driver for the device to be handled using the Google USB driver, and you may have to modify the `adb_usb.ini` file (on Mac too) for the device to be considered as an ADB compatible device.

Getting ready for test development on an iOS device

If you carefully went through all these Android steps, especially on Windows, you will hopefully be amused by the brevity of this section! There is a catch though; you can't really test on an iOS device from LiveCode. We'll look at what you have to do instead in a moment, but first, we'll look at the steps required to test an app in the iOS simulator.

Time for action – using the iOS simulator

The initial steps are much like what we did for Android apps, but the process becomes a lot quicker in later steps. Remember, this only applies to a Mac OS; you can only do these things on Windows if you are using a Mac OS in a virtual machine, which may have performance issues. This is most likely not covered by the Mac OS's user agreement! In other words, get a Mac OS if you intend to develop for iOS. The following steps will help you achieve that:

1. Open LiveCode and create a new **Mainstack** and save the stack to your hard drive.

2. Select **File** and then **Standalone Application Settings...**.

3. Click on the iOS icon to select the **Build for iOS** checkbox.

4. Close the settings dialog box and take a look at the **Test Target** menu under **Development**.

5. You will see a list of simulator options for iPhone and iPad and different versions of iOS.

6. To start the iOS simulator, select an option and click on the **Test** button.

What just happened?

This was all it took for us to get the testing done using the iOS simulators! To test on a physical iOS device, we need to create an application file first. Let's do that.

Appiness at last!

At this point, you should be able to create a new Mainstack, save it, select either iOS or Android in the Standalone Settings dialog box, and be able to see simulators or virtual devices in the Development/Test menu item. In the case of an Android app, you will also see your device listed if it is connected via USB at the time.

Time for action – testing a simple stack in the simulators

Feel free to make things that are more elaborate than the ones we have made through these steps! The following instructions make an assumption that you know how to find things by yourself in the object inspector palette:

1. Open LiveCode, create a new Mainstack, and save it someplace where it is easy to find in a moment from now.

2. Set the card window to the size 480 x 320 and uncheck the **Resizable** checkbox.

3. Drag a label field to the top-left corner of the card window and set its contents to something appropriate. `Hello World` might do.

4. If you're developing on Windows, skip to step 11.

5. Open the **Standalone Application Settings** dialog box, click on the iOS icon, and click on the **Build for iOS** checkbox.

6. Under **Orientation Options**, set the **iPhone Initial Orientation** to **Landscape Left**.

7. Close the dialog box.

8. Navigate to the **Development | Test Target** submenu and choose an iPhone Simulator.

9. Select **Test** from the **Development** menu.

10. You should now be able to see your test stack running in the iOS simulator!

11. As discussed earlier, launch the Android virtual device.

12. Open the Standalone Application Settings dialog box, click on the Android icon, and click on the **Build for Android** checkbox.

13. Under **User Interface Options**, set the **Initial Orientation** to **Landscape**.

14. Close the dialog box.

15. If the virtual device is running by now, do whatever it takes to get past the locked home screen, if that's what it is showing.

16. From the **Development/Test Target** submenu, choose the **Android emulator**.

17. Select **Test** from the **Development** menu.

18. You should now see your test stack running in the Android emulator!

What just happened?

All being well, you just made and ran your first mobile app on both Android and iOS! For an encore, we should try this on physical devices only to give Android a chance to show how easy it can be done. There is a whole can of worms we didn't open yet that has to do with getting an iOS device configured, so that it can be used for testing. This is covered in depth later in *Chapter 7, Deploying to Your Device*, which you can read now or you could visit the iOS Provisioning Portal at `https://developer.apple.com/ios/manage/overview/index.action` and look at the **How To** tab in each of the different sections.

Time for action – testing a simple stack on devices

Now, let's try running our tests on physical devices. Get your USB cables ready and connect the devices to your computer.

Lets go through the steps for an Android device first:

1. You should still have Android selected in **Standalone Application Settings**.

2. Get your device to its home screen past the initial Lock screen if there is one.

3. Choose **Development/Test Target** and select your Android device. It may well say "Android" and a very long number.

4. Choose **Development/Test**.

5. The stack should now be running on your Android device.

Now, we'll go through the steps to test a simple stack on an iOS device:

1. If you have not read *Chapter 7, Deploying to Your Device*, on how to deploy the current environment to your device or the Apple pages or have not installed certificates and provisioning files, you will have to skip this test for now.

2. Change the **Standalone Application Settings** back to **iOS**.

3. Under **Basic Application Settings** of the iOS settings is a **Profile** drop-down menu of the provisioning files that you have installed. Choose one that is configured for the device you are going to test.

4. Close the dialog box and choose **Save as Standalone Application...** from the **File** menu.

5. In **Finder**, locate the folder that was just created and open it to reveal the app file itself. As we didn't give the stack a sensible name, it will be named **Untitled 1**.

6. Open Xcode, which is in the Developer folder you installed earlier, in the Applications subfolder.

7. In the Xcode folder, choose **Devices** from the **Window** menu if it isn't already selected.

8. You should see your device listed. Select it and if you see a button labeled **Use for Development**, click on that button.

9. Drag the app file straight from the **Finder** menu to your device in the **Devices** window. You should see a green circle with a + sign. You can also click on the + sign below **Installed Apps** and locate your app file in the **Finder** window. You can also replace or delete an installed app from this window.

10. You can now open the app on your iOS device!

What just happened?

In addition to getting a test stack to work on real devices, we also saw how easy it is, once it's all configured, to test a stack, straight on an Android device. If you are developing an app that is to be deployed on both Android and iOS, you may find that the fastest way to work is to test with the iOS Simulator for iOS tests, but for this, you need to test directly on an Android device instead of using the Android SDK virtual devices.

Have a go hero – Nook

Until recently, the Android support for the Nook Color from Barnes & Noble wasn't good enough to install LiveCode apps. It seems to have improved though and could well be another worthwhile app store for you to target.

Investigate about the sign up process, download their SDK, and so on. With any luck, some of the processes that you've learned while signing up for the other stores will also apply to the Nook store. You can start the signing up process at

`https://nookdeveloper.barnesandnoble.com.`

Further reading

The SDK providers, Google and Apple, have extensive pages of information on how to set up development environments, create certificates and provisioning files, and so on. The information covers a lot of topics that don't apply to LiveCode, so try not to get lost! These URLs would be good starting points if you want to read further:

`http://developer.android.com/`

`http://developer.apple.com/ios/`

Summary

Signing up for programs, downloading files, using command lines all over the place, and patiently waiting for the Android emulator to launch—it could take the best part of a day to work through what we've covered in this chapter! Fortunately, you only have to go through it once.

In this chapter, we worked through a number of tasks that you have to do before you create a mobile app in LiveCode. We had to sign up as an iOS developer before we could download and install Xcode and iOS SDKs. We then downloaded and installed the Android SDK and configured LiveCode for devices and simulators.

We also covered some topics that will be useful once you are ready to upload a finished app. We showed you how to sign up for the Android Market and Amazon Appstore.

There will be a few more mundane things that we have to cover at the end of the book, but not for a while! Next up, we will start to play with some of the special abilities of mobile devices.

3

Building User Interfaces

So many different screens!

When making utility or game applications for desktop computers, you can often get away with having a particular sized window for which you can make custom graphics that exactly fit. With mobile devices, you have to cope with a wide range of screen sizes and aspect ratios and also have to interface elements that look correct for the operating system on the user's device.

LiveCode is capable of publishing on Mac, Windows, and Linux and goes some way toward solving the difficulty of making interface elements look right for each platform. The **View** menu has a **Look and Feel** menu item where you can choose between **Native Theme**, **Mac OS Classic**, **Windows 95**, and **Motif**. The same isn't true for mobile operating systems as all controls look like Motif. You still have two choices though: you can create graphics that look like they belong in your target OS, or you can call native routines in order to let the system itself present the appropriate controls.

In this chapter, we will:

- ◆ Set up a *test bed* mobile application
- ◆ Open an e-mail and browser windows
- ◆ Show a date picker control
- ◆ Load pictures from the library and camera
- ◆ Make an iOS styled button
- ◆ Manually lay out an interface
- ◆ Use code to lay out an interface
- ◆ Look at a powerful mobile interface control's add-on

Setting up a test bed mobile app

As a proving ground for the things we're going to try, we'll set up a single mobile app that has multiple screens, one for each of the things we want to test.

What should we call the test bed app? We could call it almost anything, but we'll let the iPhone make the decision for us. On the iPhone and iPod touch, there is only a small amount of space under the home screen icons for the name to appear. iOS will take your nice long app name and show a shortened version of the name, using ellipses to concatenate the ends of the name together. My super duper app will appear as My sup...app, not quite as informative! The number of letters that can appear without the text being truncated will vary depending on the width of the letters used, but typically, it has a limit of 11 letters. So, we will call the test bed app LC Test Bed, which is exactly 11 letters!

Time for action – making the test bed stack

Before we create the iOS and Android apps, we should get what we want ready, as a LiveCode stack and fully test it on our desktop computers. The following steps are going to assume that you know how to do what is asked in LiveCode, without precise instructions.

1. Open LiveCode, create a new **Mainstack**, and save it as `LCTestBed`.

2. Set the screen size to 320 x 480. This is just to make sure that things appear on the smallest of screens. The things we will make, will appear at the upper-left corner area of the larger screens.

3. We are going to make a button for each card in the stack; let's start by making a card named **Menu**.

4. Add buttons for **Email**, **Browser**, **DatePicker**, and **Picture**. Make sure that the buttons are big enough to touch on your devices. You should have something like what is shown here:

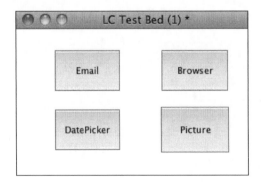

5. Create four new cards and name each one so that they match the button names.

6. Back at the first card, set the script of each button to go to the matching cards with this script:

```
on mouseUp
go card the short name of me
end mouseUp
```

7. On each card, create a button to return to the Menu card. Name the button `Menu`. Set its script to the same as the other buttons.

8. Select the Run (browse) tool and try clicking on the buttons to jump to the four cards and back to the menu.

What just happened?

Well, nothing too exciting! However, you should now have five cards and the ability to go in and out of the Menu card. We're going to add scripts to each card to help illustrate its various features. The most efficient approach will be to add all the scripts and related buttons and fields and then to test the final test bed app in one go. However, where's the fun in that! Instead, we'll go one feature at a time...

Invoking the desktop e-mail application

There are many cases where you may want to hear from the users of your applications. Perhaps, you want them to e-mail suggested improvements or to ask you questions. You could easily launch their e-mail program and leave the user to figure out what to write. Alternately, you could set the **To** address, **Subject**, and even some of the **Body** of the message. At the very least, it would make your life easier because you could filter incoming e-mails based on something that you placed in the Subject field.

Time for action – calling the native e-mail application

In the following steps we'll make some fields and a button to try sending an e-mail feature:

1. Go to the **Email** card and create four fields. Name them **To**, **CC**, **Subject**, and **Body**.

2. Make a button named **Test**.

3. In the **Test** button, add this script:

```
on mouseUp
  put field "To" into toText
  put field "CC" into ccText
  put field "Subject" into subjectText
  put field "Body" into bodyText
  revMail toText,ccText,subjectText,bodyText
end mouseUp
```

4. Select the **Run** tool and type in example information in each of the fields.

5. After setting up the **Standalone Application Settings...** and selecting the **Test Target**, click on the **Test** button.

What just happened?

One neat thing about the LiveCode syntax is that the code for mobile also works for desktop applications and vice versa. All being well, when you click on the Test button, you will find yourself in your default e-mail application ready to send the message that you had entered in the LiveCode stack fields.

Installing the e-mail test on devices

It's no great surprise that the desktop test worked. The ability to open other applications is the basic feature of LiveCode. Still, it's neat to send over some initial text for the new message to take on. Next, we should check whether this works on devices too.

Time for action – trying the test bed stack on devices

Connect your Android and/or iOS device to your computer using USB. These instructions are almost the same as in the previous chapter, when we tested a "Hello World" stack. After this point, any directions will be briefer and based on the assumption that you know the steps needed to test an app on your device. *Chapter 7*, *Deploying to Your Device*, describes all the options in the **Standalone Applications Settings** dialog. For the moment, we're only going to fill in a few details, so here, we will just view a portion of the dialog, starting with the Android settings:

1. Make sure that **Android** is checked in the **Standalone Application Settings** dialog.

2. In the **Identifier** field, type in an identifier that will be unique; `com.yourname. lctestbed` would do.

3. Get your device to its home screen past the initial lock screen if there is one.

4. In LiveCode, choose **Development/Test Target** and select your Android device. It will be named as **Android** followed by a long number.

5. Choose the **Development/Test** option.

6. After compilation, the stack should run on your Android device and you should be able to touch the **Email** button and perform a test message that will use the Android e-mail application.

On iOS, if you haven't already done so, read *Chapter 7, Deploying to Your Device*, on how to deploy to your device. At least read the parts that show you how to install your iOS developer certificates and provisioning files. As with Android, we're only going to alter a couple of items in the Standalone Application Settings. The following is the screenshot of the dialog that we'll be altering:

Perform the following steps for an iOS device:

1. Change the **Standalone Application Settings** to **iOS**.

2. Under **Basic Application Settings** of the iOS settings is a **Profile** drop-down menu of the provisioning files that you have installed. Choose the one that is configured for the device you are going to test the app on.

3. In the **Internal App ID** field, type in a unique ID. As with Android, `com.yourname.lctestbed` would do. `yourname` would of course be your name or your company name.

4. If you are testing on iPad, select the **iPod, iPhone and iPad** option from the **Supported Devices** drop-down menu.

5. Close the dialog and choose **Save as Standalone Application...** from the **File** menu.

6. When the saving is done, you may see a warning message telling you about missing splash screens and icons. It won't matter for now.

7. In **Finder**, locate the folder that was just created and open it to reveal the app file itself.

8. Open **Xcode** and choose **Devices** from the **Window** menu.

9. You should see your device listed. Select it and if you see a button labeled **Use for Development**, click on that button.

10. Drag the app file straight from the **Finder** window to your device in the **Organizer** window.

11. The small colored circle next to the device will turn orange for a moment and then back to green.

12. You can now open the app and try the **Email** button and test message, which will use the standard iOS Mail application.

What just happened?

We went through the steps needed to install the test bed app on both Android and iOS devices. We also had to change a couple of things in the standalone application settings. As you saw, there are quite a lot of settings in there. You can look forward to learning about them all in *Chapter 7, Deploying to Your Device*!

Opening a web page

Another requirement in your applications is being able to present additional online information. You want the user to click on a link, or touch as the case may be, so that he/she is taken to a page that lists all the other applications that the user can buy from you!

Time for action – calling the native browser application

This next test will go faster, or at least, the instructions will be briefer, as we will condense some of the steps in more concise directions, as given here:

1. Copy the **Test** button on the **Email** card and paste it on the **Browser** card, just to save you some time making the button look nice.

2. Edit the **Test** button script and change it to this:

```
on mouseUp
   launch url "http://www.runrev.com/"
end mouseUp
```

3. Choose the **Run** tool and click on the **Test** button. You will see the RunRev home page in your default browser.

The steps for trying the app on devices is exactly the same as with the steps to test the e-mail feature. For Android:

1. Select Android in the **Standalone Application Settings**.

2. Select your Android device as the test target from the **Development** menu (most likely, it will still be selected from before).

3. Select **Test** from the **Development** menu.

4. The previous test of the app will be overwritten and the new version will be launched automatically.

5. Try clicking on the **Browser** button and the **Test** button that you just created on the Browser card. The `http://runrev.com/` page should be opened if you click on them.

For iOS:

1. Select iOS in the standalone application settings.

2. Redo **Save as Standalone Application** and then drag the app file on your device in the **Organizer** window of Xcode, as you did the first time.

3. Try the **Browser** and **Test** buttons; you should see that the RunRev home page has opened inside Safari.

What just happened?

As with the Email test, adding the standard code to open a web page works for Android and iOS just as it does for a desktop computer.

If you are testing on both Android and iOS, you will notice that the behavior is different when you return after looking at a web page. With Android, you can press the back arrow button and still be on the Browser card of your stack. With iOS, the stack is restarted when you return. We will examine a solution later, where we write data to an external file, so that when the app is reopened, we can return the user before leaving the app.

The mobile-only date picker

The next couple of examples we will try are the ones that only work on mobile devices and not on desktop computers.

Time for action – displaying a date picker

Many applications require the user to choose a date for an event, and with mobile devices, there is a particular look to the date picker that you are shown. Using LiveCode let's us display such a control:

1. Copy the **Test** button from the Browser card and paste it on the DatePicker card.

2. Edit the script to make it like this:

```
on mouseUp
iphonePickDate "date"
end mouseUp
```

3. Select the **Run** tool and try the **Test** button. You'll see an error because this is a mobile-only feature.

4. For a change, select **iPhone** or **iPad Simulator** from the **Development/Test Target** menu and then choose **Test** from the **Development** menu.

5. You will see your stack open in the iOS simulator and you can try the **DatePicker** and **Test** buttons to then see the iOS date picker displayed.

6. Perform the same old Save As and install using the Organizer window steps to try the date picker on your iOS device.

7. Touch the **DatePicker** button on the menu card and the **Test** button on the Datepicker card. An iOS native date picker should appear.

What just happened?

Hopefully, you're getting better and are able to build and install mobile apps faster by now! In addition to testing again on a device, we also tried out the simulator. Generally speaking, it is faster to use the iOS simulator whenever you can, and only test on a device when you're checking things such as multi-touch, accelerometer, and camera support.

Time for action – loading pictures for a mobile device

Maybe one day it will be possible for us to bring in images from the user's desktop computer photo application or from their web camera, but for now, these features only work on mobile devices.

LiveCode can call upon the native photo library and camera apps. We will test both of these on Android and iOS, but of course, only if your device has some saved images and a camera. For Kindle Fire, which doesn't have a camera, make sure that you save some pictures in the Gallery app, so that we can at least try loading those. Follow these steps to load pictures for a mobile device:

1. Copy the **Test** button from the `DatePicker` card and paste it twice on the Pictures card. Change the name of the buttons to Test Camera and Test Library.

2. Edit the script of the test camera button to be:
```
on mouseUp
mobilePickPhoto "camera"
end mouseUp
```

3. Edit the script of the test library button to be:
```
on mouseUp
mobilePickPhoto "library"
end mouseUp
```

4. As we test the loading of pictures, the image that is loaded will lie on top of the test buttons, stopping us from returning to the menu card. To solve this issue, add this to the card script:

```
on mouseUp
if word 1 of the target is "image" then delete the target
end mouseUp
```

5. Go in the **Standalone Application Settings** and select **Android**.

6. We have to ask the Android OS permission to use the camera and store the image, so check the boxes for **Camera** and **Write External Storage**:

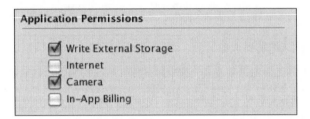

7. Repeat the steps for testing on your Android device, or installing on your iOS device.

8. Once the app is running on your device, touch **Pictures** on the first screen and then **Test Library**. You should see typical OS-specific options to choose a picture from your library or gallery.

9. The picture you have selected is loaded on the card window and will fill most of the screen, obscuring our test and menu buttons. The card script we entered gives you the ability to touch the image in order to delete it so that you can then try another test.

10. Try the **Test Camera** button. You will see the OS-specific camera application and when you have taken a picture and touched the **Use** or **Ok** button in the camera application, the image will be placed on the Pictures card.

What just happened?

These simple scripts illustrate how LiveCode is able to call the OS-specific applications to do what would otherwise take a lot of coding. What's more, as later iOS and Android OS versions are released, the same simple scripts activate the more advanced features that Apple and Google will have implemented.

Pop quiz – getting the big picture

Q1. We take so much for granted when it comes to improvements in technology. You might feel hard done by if your phone's camera is a measly 2 megapixels, but think back to how things were long ago and how big a picture you were used to seeing. In terms of the number of pixels, how many original Macintosh screens can fit in the area shown by a single 8 megapixel photo?

1.   4

2.   15

3.   24

4.   45

Answer: 45!

The original Mac had a screen that was 512 x 342 pixels. This will fit more than 45 times in the area of an 8 megapixel photo.

Making OS-styled buttons

It's nice that LiveCode can call upon an OS's native controls, but this raises a problem because the standard Motif-styled buttons will look ugly when used with the OS buttons. We can fix this either using built-in features of LiveCode or with the use of an add-on product.

Using bitmaps

As we saw in *Chapter 1*, *LiveCode Fundamentals*, you can use different bitmaps for the button's states. You could get such images by taking screenshots of the buttons on your mobile device, at least with the iOS and Android OS v4 and later versions, or you can save a lot of time by downloading files that others have made available. Some of these files are only licensed for use in prototypes; here, we'll take a look at one of the files that is also licensed to be used in commercial products.

Time for action – using Photoshop to prepare button states

The file we are going to use has Photoshop filter effects that other programs cannot handle, so unfortunately, you will need Photoshop to follow all of these steps or at least have a friend who has Photoshop! Pixelmator and GraphicConverter on Mac OS X can also extract graphics from the file, possibly, by just copying an area of the screen.

1. Read the following article:

```
http://spin.atomicobject.com/2011/03/07/photoshop-template-for-
ios-buttons/
```

2. The article points to some other sources of information; for now though, download the following file:

```
http://spin.atomicobject.com/assets/2011/3/7/iOS_Buttons.psd
```

3. Open the file in Photoshop (it may open automatically).

4. In the Layers palette, hide the layers named Background and Tool Bar – Retina.

5. Expand the layer named **Bar Button – Retina**, and hide the **Button Label** layer.

6. Use the Marquee tool to select an area around the upper-right-hand side button. It should all look like this:

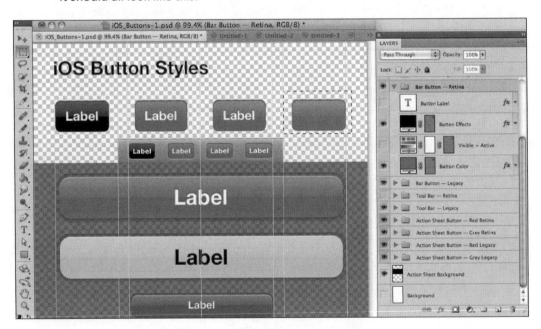

7. Choose **Copy Merged** from the **Edit** menu.

8. Select **New** from the **File** menu and make sure that the **Background Contents** property is set to **Transparent** and accept the size you are given.

9. Paste the content, it will be an exact fit, and you will see the idle state for that button.

10. Choose **Save for Web & Devices...** from the **File** menu.

11. In the save dialog, select **24 bit PNG** and make sure that the **Transparency** box is checked. Save the PNG with a suitable name, say `bluebuttonup.png`.

12. Return to the main document and turn on the Visible = Active layer.

13. Do another **Copy Merged | New | Paste | Save for Web & Devices...**.

14. Save the PNG as `bluebuttondown.png`.

15. Go back to LiveCode.

16. Reopen the test bed stack.

17. Use **File**, **Import As Control**, and **Image File...** to bring the two PNGs in the stack.

18. You can place the two images anywhere. Uncheck **Visible** in **Basic Properties** for each image.

19. Add a new button to the first card and give it the name Location.

20. Set the button script to:

```
on mouseUp
   iphoneStartTrackingLocation
   put iphoneCurrentLocation() into theLocation
   answer theLocation["latitude"]
end mouseUp
```

21. Select the Location button and in **Basic Properties** of the **Inspector** palette, turn off **Show name** and **Opaque**.

22. In **Icons & Border**, turn off **Three D**, **Border** and **Hilite border**.

23. Click on the magic wand button next to the **Icon** entry in the **Inspector** palette.

24. From the **Image library** drop-down menu, select **This Stack**.

25. Click on the lighter one of the two blue images.

26. Click on the magic wand button next to the **Hilite icon** entry and then click on the darker of the two images.

27. Resize the button just big enough to show the blue image without it being cropped.

28. Place a Label field on top of the button.

29. In **Basic Properties**, check the **Disabled** box. This is to make sure that the field doesn't trap the click you are going to perform. We want the button to get that click.

30. In **Contents**, enter `Location`.

31. Under **Text Formatting**, set the field to use **Helvetica Neue, 18 point, Bold, and center aligned**.

32. Under Colors & Palettes, set the text color white.

33. Align the field and the button so that the two are centered on each other.

34. If you now test using the iOS Simulator and click on the Location button, you will just see a zero, but trying on a device should display your latitude when you touch the button (you will have to give permission to the app to know your location the first time you press the button.)

 Note that the example is in the iOS 6 format. iOS 8 can be found at: `http://www.teehanlax.com/tools/iphone/`

What just happened?

Although the button we made, may not be of the perfect size or even have the correct look for a standalone iOS button, we did go through all of the steps that you would need to make button state images. Placing a LiveCode field over the image buttons doesn't necessarily give it the best appearance. In reality, you would take more time in Photoshop to make a button of the right width for the label you're using and might also have to add the text to the image itself. It would look better and would not need a field to show the button's name in LiveCode.

LiveCode is able to use code to create the images we need, by setting the points of a graphic and its `fillGradient`. However, once you have the component parts needed to simulate a button or other kind of control, it would still take a lot more scripting to manage these elements.

There is an easy way out, although, it will cost you $50!

Pop quiz – the cost of things these days

Q1. With the increase in your expectations about the size of a digital photo, you also expect to get a lot more for your money these days. While you weigh up the advantages of spending $50, how much better value do you think a computer's memory is now, compared to 25 years ago?

1. 10 times better

2. Half as good

3. 100 times better

4. 20,000 times better!

Answer: 4

Yes indeed. 25 years ago, Apple was selling a 4 MB add-on kit for Macintosh II for about $1,500. They now sell a 64 GB add-on for Mac Pro for $1,200.

MobGUI to the rescue!

RunRev is based in Edinburgh, Scotland, and they're a talented bunch! However, they're not the only talented Scottish folk, there's John Craig as well. He has developed a powerful add-on to LiveCode that includes an increasingly long list of iOS- and Android-OS-like controls. If you were to buy his product, you would have to pay $50 for which you get the current version plus any updates that are released in the 12 months following your purchase date. While we take a look at it here, we can also use a trial version of the product.

Time for action – getting started with MobGUI

As with the other add-ons to LiveCode, MobGUI needs to be installed in the LiveCode plugins folder. On Windows, this will be at `My Documents/My LiveCode/Plugins`. On Mac, it will be at `~/Documents/My LiveCode/Plugins`. This default location can be changed under the **LC Preferences** menu and **Files & Memory**. The following steps will guide you through getting started with MobGUI:

1. Download the latest version of MobGUI from `http://mobgui.com/download.php`.

2. The `.zip` file will expand to become a LiveCode stack named **MobGUI_V1-28. livecode** for the current version. Hopefully, there will be a newer version when you download this.

3. Drag the stack into the plugins folder and reopen LiveCode.

4. Make a new Mainstack.

5. From the **Development** menu, choose **Plugins/revMobGUI**. This window will appear when you do so:

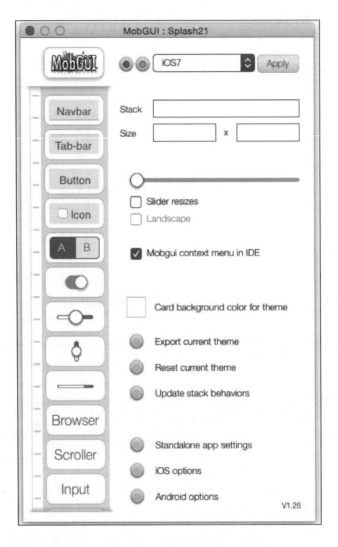

6. The MobGUI window is much like a combination of the LiveCode Tool palette and Inspector palette.

7. Try dragging different items on the card and look at the options for each item.

8. The left-hand side list is scrollable and shows additional controls.

9. Once the controls are placed on the card, they can be manipulated like the normal LiveCode controls.

10. The selection field at the top right-hand side allows different themes to be selected. Select the **android** theme and click on **Apply**. Note that the controls you dragged out change. At the time of writing this book, the **android** theme represents the older pre-Lollipop themes.

11. After you have manipulated a stack, you can export the current theme for later use. You need to save the newly created stack named the **MobGUI Theme** stack. When opened later, this stack will have an **Import** button.

What just happened?

One remarkable thing about LiveCode is that the many windows and palettes that you use in the program are all just stacks, and we've started to make use of a rather specialized stack that is going to save us a lot of time and will give us a nice interface like the OS-specific interface.

A test bed app, the MobGUI way

We're going to make much the same test bed app, but this time, we'll try to give a more iOS-like look to the app.

Time for action – using MobGUI to make a test bed app

As you work in LiveCode starting new stacks, closing others, and opening previously saved stacks, these actions can still occupy memory. Sometimes, you can get in a confused state where you're making a new Untitled stack only to find out there's still an Untitled stack on the go, which you're asked about if you want to purge. So, why not treat yourself to a quit and start a fresh launch of LiveCode! The following steps will help you achieve that:

1. Create a new Mainstack. Set the name to MGTestBed and save it somewhere you can easily find it. Perhaps, in the folder with the LCTestBed stack, which was feeling lonely!

2. Open the MobGUI window by selecting **Development/Plugins/revMobGUI**.

3. In the MobGUI window's page of controls, select the **Slider resizes** box and move the slider to select a size of **320x480**. This is the size of the original iPhone. Note the other sizes available. The card can also be resized with the LiveCode Inspector.

> Add preOpenCard code to card script

4. Select the **MobGUI context menu in IDE** option in the MobGUI window. This will enable you to edit the MobGUI control behaviors later.

5. Using the **Card Inspector**, set the name of this first card to Email.

6. Drag a **TabBar** on the card window. Click on **Snap to bottom** of the card window. It will also resize the width of the card.

7. In the MobGUI window, drag a button in the card window on top of the TabBar. Duplicate the button 3 times by holding the *Alt/option* key and dragging it. Align the four buttons and distribute them across the card using LiveCode's **Align Tools** in the **Inspector** palette.

8. Select each button and set their names and labels to `Email`, `Browser`, `DatePicker`, and `Picture`. Then, resize the buttons so that they fit their name text appropriately.

9. Select the **Email** button and choose **Object Script** from the **Object** menu or right-click on the button and choose the **Edit Script** option. The script will already look like the following screenshot:

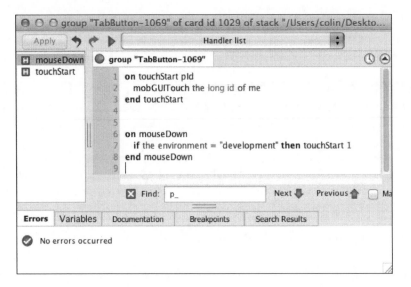

10. Add the following `mouseUp` handler to the script

```
on mouseUp
   go card the short name of me
end mouseUp
```

11. You can copy the mouseUp script of the first button and paste the script in the other three buttons. Note that there is a **preOpenControl** handler created by MobGUI following the mouseUp script in each of these buttons. Do not change that!

12. We'll need these elements on all of the four cards we're going to make, so choose the **Select All** option and then choose **Group Selected** from the **Object** menu.

13. Make sure that the group is selected and in the regular LiveCode Inspector palette, check the **Behave like a background** box.

14. Make three more cards and name them Browser, DatePicker, and Picture.

15. From the LiveCode palette, drag a Label control on the card window for each of the four cards and set the name to match the card's name.

16. In **Standalone Application Settings**, choose either iOS or Android, depending on the device you want to test on.

17. Set the **Internal App ID** or **Identifier** to com.yourname.MGTestBed.

18. If you're performing the same in iOS, make sure that you choose a profile from the Profile drop-down menu.

19. You can now do a test from the **Development** menu, but first you have to choose either **iPhone Simulator** or your connected Android device.

What just happened?

It seemed like quite a few steps, but it doesn't take much time. We already have the navigation between the four cards and an authentic iOS-like interface.

Let's get some of the test features going, but in a more native, integrated way than before.

MobGUI native controls

One powerful feature of MobGUI is that it can use ordinary LiveCode controls as placeholders for what will become native controls when you run the app on a device. This isn't something that you can't do for yourself with code, but being able to move placeholder controls around, until you like the layout, would save a lot of time.

Time for action – using native controls from MobGUI

MobGUI allows you to switch between the native control theme for iOS and Android or to redefine your own themes.

1. Right-click on the little image of the iPhone in the MobGUI window and make sure that you're on the Native iOS controls set.

2. Go to the Email card and drag 3 **Input** text controls from the MobGUI window and one **Multiline** text control.

3. Name the **Input** controls as To, CC, and Subject and the **Multiline** text control as Body. You can also add some regular LiveCode Label fields alongside the input fields as an indicator of what to enter. Size the Body field big enough to enter a few lines of text. Also, add some background color to the fields or the card so that the fields are seen properly.

4. As you make each field, note that you can set the keyboard type as well. Set it to Email for the To and CC fields.

5. From the iOS Controls 1 set, drag two buttons on the card window. Name one Done and the other Send. You should have a screenshot like this after this step:

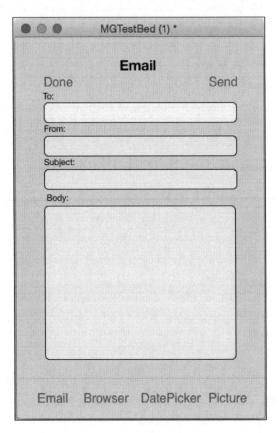

6. When we test the app and touch one of the fields, the keyboard overlay appears. We'll use the Done button as a way to hide the keyboard. Add a focus line to the `mouseUp` handler of the Done button script:

```
on mouseUp
  focus on nothing
end mouseUp
```

7. MobGUI can retrieve properties from these native fields using the `mgText` property. Change the Send button's `mouseUp` handler to use this property for each field and also, to call the `revMail` function:

```
on mouseUp
  put the mgText of group "To"" into totext
  put the mgText of group "CC"" into cctext
  put the mgText of group "Subject"" into subjecttext
  put the mgText of group "Body"" into bodytext
  revMail totext,cctext,subjecttext,bodytext
end mouseUp
```

8. Go to the Browser card.

9. From the MobGUI window, drag a **Input** control to the card window and name it URL.

10. Drag a **Browser** control to the card window and name it `Page`.

11. Adjust the sizes so that the text field fills the width of the card and the browser control fills the area between the text field and the tab bar at the bottom.

12. Select the **Browser** control and in the MobGUI window, enter a value for **URL** or use the default one already there. This will make the browser control load this URL as its first page.

13. Edit the script of the URL text field and add this handler, which looks for a Return key to go to the URL:

```
on inputReturnKey
  mobileControlSet "Page","", "url", the mgText of me
end inputReturnKey
```

14. Try another test and go to the Email and Browser cards to see them in action.

What just happened?

We recreated the first two tests from our earlier test bed app, only now, it looks a lot nicer! Also, we made use of MobGUI's ability to get and set data in native iOS controls, in this case, using the `mgText` property and `mobileControlSet`.

Note that all MobGUI controls show up as **groups** in the LiveCode Inspector and as **Custom controls** in the Project Browser. These groups are made of customized LiveCode controls such as buttons, fields, and so on. MobGUI also adds a MobGUI card to the end of your stack. This card includes invisible buttons that have behaviors defined. Behaviors are methods to create common functionality between objects without duplicating the scripts. You can view these behavior scripts by clicking on the script button on the right-hand side of the Project Browser, when you display the MobGUI card. Unless you have a specific need to change these, just leave them alone.

Have a go hero – other tests and pretty icons

Go ahead and add the other two tests to the stack in the same manner as we did in the *Time for action* sections earlier in this chapter. For the `DatePicker` example, you could examine the **Dictionary** definition for `iPhonePickDate` to see examples of how to use the picked date data in the same manner as the previous sections for example, adjustments for different screen sizes.

So far, we have tested the size using the Portrait orientation with just an iPhone. You may want to use the same stack for iPhone and iPad or perhaps, iPad and an Android tablet, which have quite different aspect ratios.

Even if you just stick with the iPhone, you would still want to take care of Portrait and Landscape. We therefore, have to find ways to arrange the many controls on the card, so that they look their best on each screen size and orientation.

There are several ways to achieve this. First, we'll look at how to use a resize handler.

Laying out using a resize handler

When a stack's window size changes, LiveCode sends a `resizeStack` message that we can trap in order to rearrange controls for the new width and height.

Time for action – a simple code layout example

It could get quite complicated if you did lay out all of the card's controls with code, so we're only going to construct a simple case to show the technique. You can enhance this later for more complex cases.

1. Create a new Mainstack.

2. Add four buttons across the width of the card.

3. Put this handler in the card script:

```
on resizeStack newWidth,newHeight
put the width of button 1 into buttonWidth
put (newWidth - 4 * buttonWidth)/5 into gap
put the top of button 1 into buttonTop
repeat with a = 1 to 4
    set the top of button a to buttonTop
    set the left of button a to gap + (a-1) * (gap+buttonWidth)
  end repeat
  pass resizeStack
end resizeStack
```

4. Resize the card window. The buttons should spread out evenly across the card.

5. Go to **Standalone Application Settings** and select the iOS option.

6. Make sure that the supported devices include iPad.

7. Set the orientation options to include all the four orientations.

8. From the **Development** menu, set the **Test Target** as the **iPad Simulator** and perform a Test.

9. In the simulator, choose either **Rotate Left** or **Rotate Right** from the **Hardware** menu.

10. The buttons should spread themselves out across the screen in both the portrait and landscape orientation.

What just happened?

In addition to making a simple example of how the resizeStack handler can be handled, we also saw that the changes in orientation also send the resizeStack message.

Laying out using the LiveCode Geometry Manager

While a control is selected on the card, the Inspector palette has an entry named Geometry. It's a somewhat strange interface! Let's take a look:

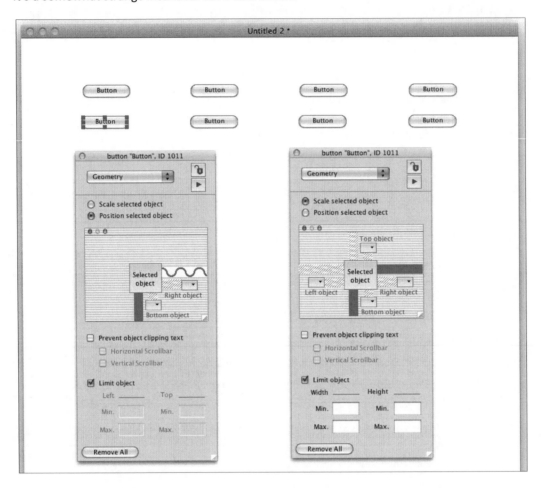

These faint horizontal and vertical bars are used to select whether you want the control to be scaled or positioned by a fixed amount or relative amount. That is, if a button is 100 pixels from the right of the card window and if you select the position a fixed amount away, then as you resize the card window, the button will remain 100 pixels away from the right edge of the window. If, on the other hand, you use the relative setting and the button is 80 percent across the card window, it will still be 80 percent across the window after you have resized it.

The first click on one of these bars will make it turn solid red in color and this indicates that it's a fixed amount away from the edge of the card. If you click on it again, it takes the shape of a red waveform, indicating that it's going to be relative.

In the screenshot, you can see that the selected button is set to a fixed amount from the bottom of the card and a relative amount from the right of the card. The image also shows the scaling settings for the control.

Note that an object can also be positioned relative to other objects. Refer to the **Right object** and **Bottom object** pop-up selectors in the preceding screenshot.

Time for action – using the Geometry Manager to position buttons

We'll add some buttons to the stack that we are currently working on:

1. Take the first four buttons and duplicate them to get another set of four buttons below the previous ones.

2. Select the first of the new buttons and in the **Geometry** section of the Inspector palette, click once on the vertical bar and twice on the horizontal bar; you will end up with the state shown in the previous screenshot.

3. Do the same for the other three buttons.

4. Try resizing the card window.

What just happened?

That was quite a quick test, and if all went well, you will see that resizing the card window includes positioning the first four buttons using the `resizeStack` handler that we added, and it's positioning of the second set of four buttons using the Geometry Manager. With the settings we used, the results should be much the same, except that the second set of four buttons will remain a fixed distance away from the bottom of the card window.

There is a lot of power in the Geometry Manager and you should take a look at the other abilities it has at the reference link shown at the end of this chapter. However, it is not the best way to deal with mobile screen sizes.

Resolution independence

LiveCode 6.5, and beyond...

One of the features listed in *Chapter 1, LiveCode Fundamentals*, has already been developed and is present in LiveCode 6.5. The new feature is Resolution Independence.

Now, after seeing the two complex ways of adjusting the screen size, you may be able to forget all of it. In LiveCode 6.5, a new feature called Resolution Independence was introduced, and the correct use of this feature will make many of the layout difficulties go away.

There are two approaches in place to help you deal with different device sizes and aspect ratios: the Multiple Density Support and the Full Screen Scaling Mode. Some of the concepts are a little tricky, but a few screenshots will hopefully make them clear!

Multiple density support

So far in this chapter, we overlooked the issue of the **DPI (dots per inch)** of devices. For Android devices, there are hundreds of different resolutions and DPI values. With iOS, there are only a few variations of DPI and resolution. The simplest these problem cases to examine, is where you want the same app to look like and work in the same manner as iPhone 3GS and iPhone 4 Retina or later versions of iPhones. Both have the same size screen, but iPhone 4's retina display has twice the DPI. This URL shows you the difference between all the current iPhones: http://www.paintcodeapp.com/news/ultimate-guide-to-iphone-resolutions.

With the MobGUI and Geometry Manager solution, you are effectively storing layout values or instructions behind the scenes that are ready to adapt to the user's device screen size. The Multiple Density Support in LiveCode 6.5 is an easier way to solve this issue.

Pixels and points

A pixel is an illuminated dot in an image or of a screen, whereas a point is a unit of measurement in print, generally, 1/72nd of an inch. If a screen has exactly 72 DPI, the two would be the same, and in the earlier days of Macintosh computers, this was pretty much the case. More modern Macs and PCs and most mobile devices are a lot more detailed than 72 DPI. With LiveCode 6.5, and its later versions, you can now make a stack that works in points, that will then fill the device screen by taking the image of each card and by applying a scaling factor to it.

While doing such scaling, something must be assumed to be of natural size. For iOS, LiveCode uses non-Retina screens as a scale factor of 1X and Retina screens are a scale factor of 2X. iPhone 5 and 6 introduced more sizes. A scale factor of 3X is required for iPhone 6 Plus. With Android, things are more complicated as it has at least seven levels of scaling factor.

In fact, really, there are an infinite number of scaling factors going on behind the scenes. However, you generally don't have to worry about them because LiveCode automatically gives you the ability to show different versions of an image depending on the DPI of the device in question.

Image naming convention

LiveCode will look at the file names of the included images (that have been added in the **Copy Files** part of the **Standalone Application Settings** dialog) and will load in the appropriately named version of the image. In the example shown here, two images have been added, `icon.png` and `icon@2x.png`. To make it easier to spot which one you are seeing, 512 and 1024 have been added to what would otherwise be two resolutions of the same icon:

This image is slightly magnified here to help you see that the 512 version of the image is lower resolution than the 1024 version.

The names used for iOS are:

◆   `imagename.ext` (for example, `flowers.png`)

◆   `imagename@2x.ext` (for example, `flowers@2x.png`)

◆   `imagename@3x.ext` (for example, `flowers@3x.png`) for iPhone 6 Plus

The first one is considered as the 1X scaled version and the `@2x` name is considered as the 2X scaled version and the same goes for the `@3x` version.

> Note that you also need to specify the appropriate **Splash Screen** files in the LiveCode **Standalone Application Settings**. Otherwise, the iPhone will use lower resolution images. This can be verified by examining the `screenRect` of the device. Even though iPhone 6 Plus has a physical resolution of 1080 x 1920, use the 3x image sizes of 1242 x 2208. The phone automatically downsizes the image. 2x images will be displayed fine on iPhone 6.

The names and scaling factors used for Android are more varied:

- `imagename@ultra-low.ext` - 0.25X
- `imagename extra-low.ext` - 0.5X
- `imagename low.ext` - 0.75
- `imagename medium.ext` - 1X
- `imagename high.ext` - 1.5X
- `imagename@extra-high.ext` - 2x
- `imagename@ultra-high.ext` - 4x

In actual practice, you may find that you only need two or three versions of an image to make an image look good enough on a wide range of DPI devices.

The full-screen scaling mode

Prior to LiveCode 6.5 and its multiple density support, you had to do all the hard work by yourself! At least now you can design for just iPhone or iPad and have Retina versions of these devices looked after by LiveCode. With Android though, you still need to have a variety of layouts or alternately, have code that would position the interface elements based on the aspect ratio and pixel dimensions of the device.

With the density support, you only have to take care of the aspect ratio, but there are still a lot of these to be taken care of. For utility-like applications, you will most likely have to go to this trouble, so that users get the expected experience. However, there are many types of applications that are more graphical and that can take advantage of the full screen scaling modes: `empty`, `exactFit`, `showAll`, `noBorder`, and `noScale`. Let's take a look at what these are...

Syntax

The general syntax, by the way, is to type this in your stack script:

```
on preopenstack
  set the fullscreenmode of the current stack to "showAll"
end preopenstack
```

The quotes are required for the four active modes. The empty mode does not need quotes.

The empty mode

If **fullscreenmode** is **empty**, the card area is changed to match the device screen. That is, the top left card is in the top-left corner of the device screen and the card width and height match the actual pixel width and height of the device. Well, except if you have taken advantage of the multiple density support discussed earlier! Essentially, empty is the existing behavior in the earlier versions of LiveCode.

The showAll mode

This mode arrived slightly later than the other modes and is present in LiveCode 6.6 and its later versions. With **showAll**, as the `fullscreenmode`, the card's contents will be scaled, so that all of it is within the device's screen. For devices that have a different aspect ratio than your card, elements that were outside of the card area are revealed. Suppose you create a graphical book app where you want the full height of the card to exactly fill the height of the device screen, but you don't want black bars down the sides on a wider device, then you could extend the background pattern beyond the left- and right-hand side of the card area. On a narrower device, such as iPad, you would see the 4:3 area of the card. On a wider device, say iPhone 5, the extra background would be revealed. The following illustration shows which area of the background image will be seen on different devices:

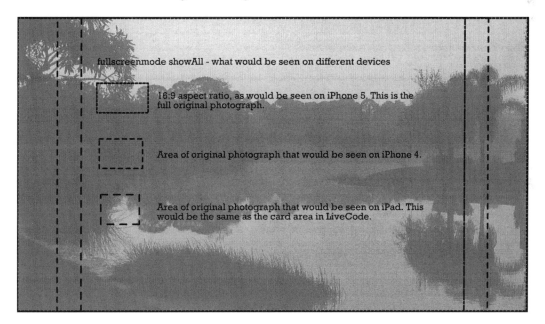

The letterbox mode

The **letterbox** mode is identical to **showAll** except that the areas beyond the card area are hidden and leave you with the typical movie letterbox effect, hence the name!

The noBorder mode

The **noBorder** mode is very useful, but takes some time to get used to. Let's say you are making a graphical adventure game, along the lines of Myst, and you want to use the same graphics for all devices. You could create a scene that has an aspect ratio of 14:9 and make sure that the important content is not too close to the edges. When the scene is viewed in the noBorder mode on an iPad, you would see the full height of the scene and most of the width. When viewed on iPhone 5, you would see the full width of the scene and most of the height. As the name suggests, the card area would be scaled, so that there are no borders, as there would be in the letterbox mode. The following illustration shows which areas of an original 14:9 photograph would be visible for a 4:3 iPad and a 16:9 iPhone:

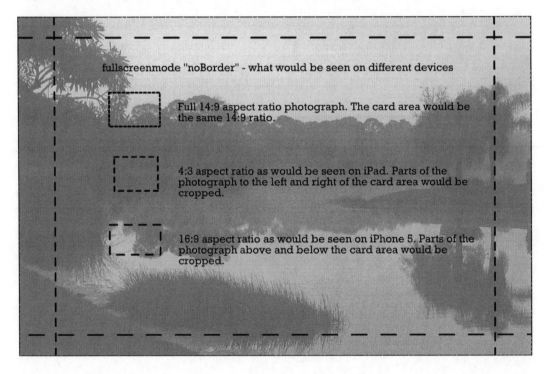

fullscreenmode "noBorder" - what would be seen on different devices

Full 14:9 aspect ratio photograph. The card area would be the same 14:9 ratio.

4:3 aspect ratio as would be seen on iPad. Parts of the photograph to the left and right of the card area would be cropped.

16:9 aspect ratio as would be seen on iPhone 5. Parts of the photograph above and below the card area would be cropped.

The exactFit mode

As the name implies, **exactFit** would take the card's content and squish it to fill the device's screen. It's hard to think of a use case for this mode, but perhaps, if you perform some sort of artistic visualizer, the squishing wouldn't matter much!

 As mentioned previously, the Geometry Manager has a lot of powerful features. If your interest is also in desktop applications, take a look at the lesson at:

```
http://lessons.runrev.com/s/lessons/m/4067/
1/19026-Geometry-Manager
```

Summary

The trick with easy-to-use tools, such as LiveCode, is to create mobile apps that users think were created with the hard-to-use native tools, such as Xcode. You can achieve this because of LiveCode's ability to call upon native features and because you can make interfaces that look appropriate.

In this chapter, we covered several ways to achieve this goal by calling native OS features using simple LiveCode commands. We prepared images to be used for button states and made buttons that look OS-specific by adding these images. We also created controls that look like iOS native controls with MobGUI and laid out the interface with code, with the Geometry Manager.

So far, these have all been small test stacks to get us warmed up! Next, we're going to look at the general application structure to make a fully fleshed out utility application.

4

Using Remote Data and Media

While creating a LiveCode application, we need to think about the structure of the stack, its code, and the data it uses. Applications can be made when all the supporting data is within the application, but quite often, we want to display data that is out in the real world somewhere and also want to save information (a high-score list perhaps) to text files that are external to the application. You may also want to share information with other people or sync between apps or devices.

In this chapter, we will:

- Look at the various ways a stack might be structured
- Think about where code should go
- Write to and read from external text files
- Create a scrapbook-like app to remember interesting Internet-based media files

Do you want to save time typing code?

There are a lot of lines of code in this chapter. The code is shown along with explanations of each function and you could use this code to build up something that matches the corresponding sample file. However, it would be very easy to make a mistake while transcribing the scripts, both in terms of what the script says and where the script should be placed. It may be safer to study the sample files and read the overall description here. You can download the code from the Packt Publishing website at https://www.packtpub.com/books/content/support.

The stack structure

There are two aspects to how the stack may be structured. One is about how user interface elements are organized and the other is about where in the hierarchy of a stack you should place your code. The first addresses how to make the app understandable, logical, and easy to use. The second addresses how to minimize development time, subsequent maintenance effort, and how to maximize the resulting performance of the app.

Code-driven and manually created layouts

When you imagine how a typical mobile application appears, it would be somewhat along these lines:

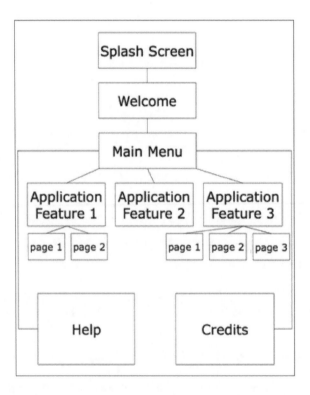

Sometimes, applications are entirely code-driven where every screen you see is created using code at the time that it's needed. Perhaps, it would already lay out the elements that are saved as resources and then the code would load these resources. In either case, the whole application could take place on the equivalent of one LiveCode card.

Another approach would be to lay out every possible screen combination as different cards or even stacks and to go to the card or stack that looks like how the app appears at that moment.

In the first case, you would need to run the application and go through the user actions in order to check whether the layout was correct. Then, you would need to go back and change the code or resources and try again. In the second case, you may face a lot of combinations of layout.

As we start making apps here, we'll try to find a middle ground where we'll use cards to set up the main screens we'll need and then we'll use code to show and hide other elements. Our goal is to try and be efficient and not create complex code to lay out items that could be laid out quickly by hand. We also don't want to use a lot of images when a small amount of code could get us the same results.

Locations for code

LiveCode is extremely flexible in terms of how you structure things that you make with it. In addition to a dozen different kinds of controls that could contain code, you can also control front scripts, groups, the current card, a mainstack, stacks in use, back script, and LiveCode itself. The following diagram shows you only a few example controls, but gives you the sense of how many levels there are to the hierarchy of LiveCode:

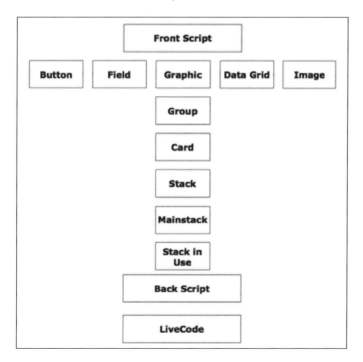

You can also have sub stacks that are often used to show dialog windows, the ability to add front and back scripts, and you can put stacks in and out of use too. Overall, it can get quite confusing!

It is largely a case of personal style as to where you put your scripts and often, you may have a reasonable argument why you did it in a certain way. You could argue that all the actions that take place should be in the script of the button you clicked on. It would make it easy to edit all the handlers involved and if you need the same features in another stack, you would only have to copy the button across. However, if you had a number of those buttons on the screen and needed to make changes, you would have to do so for all of them.

Another valid argument would be to say that all handlers are at the stack level. You would then have one central place to make changes, but you would have to make lots of if statements to check which control has been operated on.

You might want to reuse routines that you have developed over time and would have a set of stacks that you could put into use, where each stack just handles a particular aspect of the task at hand. In the world of **Object-oriented Programming (OOP)**, it's quite common to extend this approach to a crazy degree with hundreds or even thousands of small files where each file handles a tiny portion of the overall application.

We won't go to any of these extremes. Instead, we will try to put code at the lowest level that it needs to be without duplicating the code, as you make additional controls that need the same code. While doing this, we will try to think ahead and spot efficiencies that we can use. Let's look at an example.

Suppose you have a main menu button and its function is to take the user back to the card named main. Having this as the button's script would make sense:

```
on mouseUp
  go card "main"
end mouseUp
```

It would appear to be the lowest level the code can be at and we're not going to duplicate it, as there's just one main menu button. However, suppose we want to track the user's progress, the main menu button won't know anything about that. So, we could do this instead:

```
on mouseUp
  navTo "main"
end mouseUp
```

In the card script, there would be this handler:

```
on navTo aCard
  saveNavState
  go card aCard
end navTo
```

The `saveNavState` function would be somewhere, saving the user's state. The only problem is that for each of the cards we make, which includes the main menu button, we will have to have this `navTo` handler in each of their scripts. Therefore, we'll put the handler in the mainstack stack script. With it being at this level, it can handle calls from any button on any card. The help button's script could be this:

```
on mouseUp
  navTo "help"
end mouseUp
```

Going to the help card would also save the user's state. Later, we could also add a visual effect as you jump from place to place and make that change in `navTo` instead of going around the various buttons that make use of the `navTo` handler.

Pop quiz – name that structure

There is a common term used to describe the LiveCode hierarchy that helps convey how information is passed up and down the hierarchy. What is that term called?

1. The Event Horizon
2. The Message Path
3. The Call Stack
4. The Home Stack

Answer: 2

For further reading, RunRev has an online lesson that describes the message path, which you can find at:

```
http://lessons.runrev.com/s/lessons/m/4603/l/44036-the-livecode-
message-path
```

Loading and saving external data

In many applications, you will want to keep track of changes that a user has made. There are several ways to do this with LiveCode, including querying a URL, reading and writing to a text file, and saving data inside a stack.

Querying a URL

Quite often, web-based applications load and save data from server-side scripts. This can work with LiveCode apps too. Here's an example which shows the closing share price for Google yesterday:

```
put url "http://quote.yahoo.com/d/quotes.csv?s=GOOG&f=p"
```

At the moment of writing this book, this line was tested and 609.46 appeared in the **Message Box,** shown as follows:

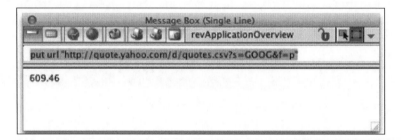

Who knows what you'll find when you try it! In fact, while doing the second revision of this book, the number that popped up was 1172.9301. Go Google!

As with any such calls to an online service, there is a chance that it may take some time for the value to return, and in the preceding example, LiveCode would be blocked from doing anything else until the data returns. An alternate approach for this, is to load the URL in order to cache it and then display the results when it is cached. LiveCode would be able to do other actions while the data returns. A button script would look like this:

```
on mouseUp
  unload url "http://quote.yahoo.com/d/quotes.csv?s=GOOG&f=p"
  load url "http://quote.yahoo.com/d/quotes.csv?s=GOOG&f=p" with
message "gotit"
end mouseUp

on gotit addr, state
  if state is "cached" or state is "downloaded" then
    answer url addr
```

```
    else
      answer state
    end if
  end gotit
```

The `gotit` handler also checks whether the call worked fine and if it didn't, it will display the error that caused the problem. The `unload` line is used to make sure that you're not reading the previously cached value. If it's a value that only changes infrequently, as with the closing price of a stock, then you would usually only clear the cached version when it's likely to be changed. For this example, that might be the next day.

Posting data works in the same way. A game that sends your score to the server can do it this way:

```
on sendscore username,score
  put url "http://www.mysite.com/hiscores/savescore.php?user=" &
username & "&score=" & score into err
  if err is not "ok" then answer err
end sendscore
```

If `username` or any other parts of the posted data contain space characters, you should use `URLEncode` in the location first. Doing so will convert spaces and other special characters into codes that will safely arrive at the destination URL. The following would be a safer variation of the preceding code:

```
on sendscore username,score
  put "http://www.mysite.com/hiscores/savescore.php?user=" & username
& "&score=" & score into tPostAddress
put url URLEncode(tPostAddress) into err
  if err is not "ok" then answer err
end sendscore
```

Reading and writing to a text file

Back in the days of HyperCard, the only real choice to save and load external data was to write a text file. LiveCode can of course do that too, and in some cases, it may be the simplest solution. Configuration and preference files are a couple of good examples where a small text file can be used to set up the application in the way the user wishes it to be.

As an example, say we have configuration text files named `englishstrings.txt` and `frenchstrings.txt` that were included in the **Copy Files** list of the **Standalone Application Settings** dialog box and they are going to be used to set the button's names in English or French within your application. Also, we'll want to write a preferences file to remember the user's choice. When the app is opened, we would check what the preferences file says and then load the appropriate strings file.

With mobile operating systems, iOS in particular, there are strict rules about where you are allowed to save data. As we move forward, we will use locations that are approved for such use by Apple and Google.

The text files that you include in a mobile app will be in the same location as the app itself, and the text files that you want to write to, should be in the `documents` folder of your app. Because these paths look quite different in iOS and Android, we should use LiveCode's `specialFolderPath` function to locate these folders. Here's how an `openStack` handler would check whether the preferences have been set and if not, would take the user to an initial language choice screen:

```
on openStack
  global langstrings
  put "file:" & specialFolderPath("documents") & "/prefs.txt" into
prefsfile
  put url prefsfile into prefstext
  if prefstext is empty then
    -- prefs have never been set, so go to the language choice card
    go card "language choice"
  else
    -- language has previously been chosen, so we load up the right
file
    put "file:" & specialFolderPath("engine") & prefstext & "strings.
txt" into langfile
    put url langfile into langstrings
  end if
end openStack
```

The special **engine** folder path is in the same location as the application file and the supporting files that you included in the **Copy Files** section of the **Standalone Application Settings** dialog box (as described in the *Copy Files* section of *Chapter 7, Deploying to Your Device*) while saving the standalone application. In the preceding example, there would be files named `englishstrings.txt`, `frenchstrings.txt`, `spanishstrings.txt`, and so on. The following line of code will concatenate the path where the included files are located, the language that you wish to use (stored in the variable `prefstext`), and the ending of these filenames:

```
put "file:" & specialFolderPath("engine") & prefstext & "strings.txt"
into langfile
```

This will give you the full path to the language strings text file that matches your chosen language.

Using another stack to store data

Ideally, you would just save changes in the stack you are in at the time, except that iOS doesn't permit you to save the changes in the application directory. We have to work around this by saving a stack, in the documents folder. The stack to save can either be the one that is our application stack or it could just be a stack purely used to store data. Saving data in a stack can be more convenient than saving it in text files. For example, you can have several text fields that are there to store bits of information that will be needed the next time the app is run. If you use text files, you would either need lots of them or you will have to process the text from a single file in order to extract the individual bits of information.

It's possible to try and save data in stacks without making a mobile app to check whether the basic technique works. Afterwards, you can try the same on an actual device. An advantage of trying this on your computer first is that you can browse to the documents folder in order to see the magic as it happens!

Time for action – creating a data save stack

We're going to make a copy of a stack, but only if another copy of that stack doesn't exist. LiveCode has a nice if there is a... function, which was made for times like this!

First, we will create the stacks we'll need by following these steps:

1. Start a new Mainstack with the name LaunchStack. Save it somewhere other than your computer's Documents folder.

2. Start another new Mainstack with the name AppStack. Save it in the same folder as the first stack.

3. Place some data on each stack's card, so that you can easily recognize when you're in that stack. For example, drag a button onto the card of the LaunchStack stack and name it in a way that makes it very easy to recognize. Do the same for the AppStack stack.

4. Put the following openStack handler in the stack script of LaunchStack:

```
on openStack
  set the defaultFolder to specialFolderPath("Documents")
  if there is not a file "AppStack.livecode" then
  put the filename of this stack into masterfile
    set the itemdelimiter to "/"
    put "AppStack.livecode" into the last item of masterfile
    --put specialFolderPath("engine") & "/AppStack.livecode" into
masterfile
```

```
      put specialFolderPath("Documents") & "/AppStack.livecode" into
appfile
      put URL ("binfile:" & masterfile) into URL ("binfile:" &
appfile)
   end if
   go stack specialFolderPath("Documents") & "/AppStack.livecode"
answer the filename of this stack
end openStack
```

5. Save both the stacks and quit LiveCode.

Before trying the stacks on a device or in the simulator, we'll try them as desktop stacks by following these steps:

1. Look in your Documents folder; there should *not* be an AppStack.livecode file in this folder at the moment.

2. Launch LiveCode by double-clicking on the LaunchStack.livecode file. If you find that LiveCode doesn't launch this way, make sure that you have the associated .livecode documents to be opened with LiveCode. If you are using more than one copy of LiveCode, say you're trying the Community version and the Commercial version, you can drag the stack file onto the copy of LiveCode that you're intending to use.

3. Look in your Documents folder; there now should be an AppStack.livecode file with the time when the file was created that matches the current time.

4. You should also see that the path to AppStack is indeed in your Documents folder.

Now, follow these steps to try our stacks on a mobile device or an iOS Simulator:

1. Close the AppStack stack and uncomment the put specialFolderPath... line from the LaunchStack stack script that you entered in step 4.

2. Go to **Standalone Application Settings** and choose the **Copy Files** section.

3. Click on **Add File...** and locate and add the original AppStack.livecode stack (not the one that was created with the previous test).

4. Choose either the **Android** or **iOS** section of the **Standalone Application Settings** and check the box to make the app available for that platform.

5. From the **Development** menu, select your test target. That would be either one of the iOS simulators, if you choose iOS, or the connected Android device.

6. Select **Test** from the **Development** menu. You should now be able to view your AppStack and an alert dialog box showing the path to the stack. The following screenshot shows the resulting dialog box in the iOS Simulator window and in an Android 4 tablet:

What just happened?

We set up our app to copy the main application stack in the documents area on the device, so that we'll be able to make changes and save those successfully. If you happen to test on iOS and Android, you will see quite different looking paths for the stack. LiveCode takes care of finding these special folders for us.

Pop quiz – other special places

Check whether you just happen to know this or use this question as an excuse to read the release notes and dictionary! Which of these is *not* a `specialFolderPath` type?

1. Users
2. Home
3. Desktop
4. 0x000e

Answer: 1

The `specialFolderPath` types `Home` and `Desktop` are not used by Android and `Desktop` is not used by iOS. `0x000e` sounds suspicious, but is actually the `specialFolderPath` entry for `My Videos` under Unix! None of the systems have a `Users` entry.

Creating a web "scraper" app

As an excuse to try out various native mobile controls, we're going to make an app that can read web pages and extract links to different media on the page. The app will have a card that shows a web browser, cards to show the links, text, media from the web page, and a set of cards to remember the selected items.

Time for action – setting up the tab navigation

Before getting into the process of making the Browser card, we need to set up the items that are shared across all the cards in the app. The following steps will help you do this:

1. We'll use MobGUI again to make life easier. Select **revMobGUI** by navigating to the **Development | Plugins** submenu. Also, open the **Project Browser** from the LiveCode **Tools** menu to observe the stack structure as it develops.

2. Create a new Mainstack, set its name to `WebScraper`, and save it someplace.

3. In these instructions, we'll use iPhone in portrait orientation, but feel free to use iPad or an Android size for the card. Either select **iOS7** and **320x480** in the MobGUI window or your preferred options.

4. As you did in the *Time for action – using MobGUI to remember layouts for us* section in *Chapter 3, Building User Interfaces*, use the MobGUI tools to add a **Navbar** and click on **Snap to top** of the card window, a **Tab-bar** with **Snap to bottom** of the card window, and **Bg colors** for both. Note that a MobGUI card and behavior controls are added to the project automatically when MobGUI controls are added to the Mainstack.

5. Drag a LiveCode field control to the NavBar and label it `NavBar`. Format it as you like.

6. Drag out a **Button** control from the MobGUI palette and duplicate it four times. Select all the five buttons and select **Align Objects** from the **Inspector**. Align their tops and distribute them across the card. Drag the five buttons to the Tab-bar that you just created and adjust their size and position as desired.

7. Name the five buttons as `Browser`, `Links`, `Text`, `Media`, and `Keepers`. Do this by setting the **Label** entry in the Inspector palette.

8. Edit the script of each button and in the `mouseUp` handler, add the following lines to leave the handler looking like this:

```
on mouseUp
  put the short Name of me into tTabText
  set the Text of field "NavBar" to tTabText
  go card tTabText
  init
end mouseUp
```

9. From the **Edit** menu, and select **Select All | Group Selected** from the **Object** menu.

10. Select the group, and in the **Basic Settings** menu of the regular LiveCode Object Inspector, give the group, the name `Common` and check the **Behave like a background** button.

11. Set the name of the card to `Browser`.

12. Make a new card and name it `Links`. Note that the grouped buttons appear on the new card.

13. Do the same for three more cards that are to be named `Text`, `Media`, and `Keepers`.

14. Go to **Standalone Application Settings**, choose **iOS** or **Android** as the platform you want to try, select the appropriate target from the **Development** menu, and perform a **Test**.

15. Click on or touch the five tab buttons and you should see that the name of the `NavBar` field has changed.

What just happened?

By naming the buttons and cards the same, we were able to go to the five cards using the script attached to the group. Also, we used the button script to set the name of the NavBar to match the name of the card we had jumped to. The `init` line will come on its own as we write the card scripts.

 Do not use the same name with the same type of control on the same card. Your script may end up operating on the wrong control.

The Browser card

We'll now add a few controls and scripts to the first card to create the following mini web browser:

The native browser control has many properties, actions, and messages associated with it. You can view both the **iOS Release Notes** and the **Android Release Notes** at the following websites:

http://downloads.livecode.com/livecode/5_5_5/LiveCodeNotes-5_5_5-iOS.pdf

http://downloads.livecode.com/livecode/5_5_5/LiveCodeNotes-5_5_5-Android.pdf

Additional updates on support documents can be found at the following :

`http://livecode.com/blog/2013/10/18/6-1-2-brings-ios-7-support/`

For our application though, we only need a few of LiveCode's abilities.

Time for action – adding the browser controls

Return to the first card of the stack and find your way to the native controls part of the MobGUI window. The following steps will guide you through it:

1. Drag the **Browser** control on the card window.

2. Resize the control to fill the width of the card and resize the control so that its height fits between the tab bar and a little way below the NavBar. Give it the name `Page`.

3. With the browser control selected, make sure that the box in the MobGUI window titled **Auto delete** is checked. This will help reduce the memory usage of the final app during the times you're not on the browser card.

4. From the MobGUI window, drag an **Input** control into the gap between the browser control and the NavBar. Name it `url` and resize it to be nearly as wide as the card, leaving space for the **Go** button on the right.

5. Drag a **Button** control into that space, set its label to `Go`, and resize it to look nice.

6. Edit the script of the **Go** button (which as you may notice, is really a group) and add a couple of lines in the mouseUp handler, as follows:

```
on MouseUp
  mobileControlSet "Page", "url", the mgText of group "url"
  focus on nothing
end mouseUp
```

7. Later, we will send an `init` message to the cards. For the Browser card, we can use this as a way to restore the previously chosen web page. Add the following to the Browser card script:

```
on init
  global gPageURL
  if gPageURL is not empty then
    set the pURL of group "Page" to gPageURL
  else
    set the pURL of group "Page" to "http://www.google.com/"
  end if
end init
```

8. Edit the script of the browser (group `Page`) control. We're going to use the `browserFinishedLoading` message to know when to update some variables and URL text.

9. Modify this handler of the browser control's script, shown as follows:

```
on browserFinishedLoading pURL,pType
   global gPageURL,gPageHTML
   put pURL into gPageURL
   put url pURL into gPageHTML
   set the mgText of group "url" to pURL
   pass browserFinishedLoading
end browserFinishedLoading
```

10. Save and perform another **Test** to see the browser card in action.

What just happened?

Setting the `pURL` command of the browser control to `mgText` was enough to make the browser function, but some of what was just done was in preparation for what we'll need in the other cards. In particular, we used the regular LiveCode `put url` command to stash a copy of the web page HTML code in a global variable and this will be needed when we start extracting links and media from the page.

The Links card

The Links, Text, and Media cards will take the page source that is stored in the `gPageHTML` global variable and extract the bits of interest from it. How will they do that?

A common approach while extracting a known pattern of text is to use regular expressions, which are often referred to as `regex` or `regexp`. At it's the simplest approach, it's easy to understand, but can get quite complex.

Read the Wikipedia article if you want to understand about a regular expression in depth at:

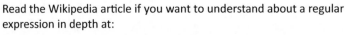
`http://en.wikipedia.org/wiki/Regular_expression`

Another useful source of information is this Packt Publishing article on regular expressions, which you can find at `http://www.packtpub.com/article/regular-expressions-python-26-text-processing.`

One problem though, is that using regexp to parse HTML content is frowned upon. There are scores of articles online telling you outright NOT TO parse HTML with regexp! Here's one pithy example at

`http://boingboing.net/2011/11/24/why-you-shouldnt-parse-html.html`.

Now, parsing an HTML source is exactly what we want to do here and one solution to the problem is to mix and match using LiveCode's other text matching and filtering abilities to do most of the work. Although it's not exactly regexp, LiveCode can use regular expressions in some of its matching and filtering functions and they are somewhat easier to understand than full-blown regexp. So, let's begin by using these.

While looking for links, we will make the assumption that the link is inside an `a href` tag, but even then, there are a lot of variations of how that can appear. The general structure of an `href` tag is like this:

```
<a href="http://www.runrev.com/support/forum/">Link text that the user
will see</a>
```

In the text of the web page will be the phrase `Link text that the user will see`. When this is pointed at by the mouse, the user will see the pointing finger cursor, and when it's clicked on, the page will reload using the URL shown in the `href` part of the tag.

The preceding example shows the full path to the support forum; here are the ways that the very same web location might be written as in a page link:

`http://www.runrev.com/support/forum/`

`/support/forum/`

`support/forum/`

`../support/forum/`

The first link will take you there no matter where you are at that time. The second will take you there if you're somewhere else on the `http://runrev.com/` site. The third will be correct while you are at the root level of `http://runrev.com/`, and the last example would work from within one of the other root-level directories on the site.

With regex, you might create an extravagant expression that deals with all possible variations of how the links are contained in the page source, but even then it would not give us the full paths we need.

By taking things slowly, we can reduce the whole page source to a set of lines of "a href" entries, extract the URL part of each line, and finally, take the preceding variations and convert them into full path URLs.

Time for action – making a links extraction function

Sometimes it's handy to create tests in a separate stack and then to take the function you've made into your application stack. The following points will help you in making a links extraction function:

1. Create a new **Mainstack** and save it, just to be safe!

2. Add a couple of fields and a button.

3. Set the button's script to this:

```
on mouseUp
   put url "http://www.runrev.com/" into field 1
   put getLinks(field 1) into field 2
end mouseUp
```

4. Edit the stack script and create a function for `getLinks`. Start with returning what it has sent:

```
function getLinks pPageSource
   return pPageSource
end getLinks
```

5. If you try clicking on the button at this point, you will see that the whole page source appears in field 2.

6. We're going to use the filter function, and it needs the text to be in separate lines. So, we want every link to be in a line of its own. The `replace` function can do this nicely. Add these two lines to the script (before the "return" line, of course!):

```
replace "/a>" with "/a>" & return in pPageSource
replace "<a" with return & "<a" in pPageSource
```

7. Try clicking on the button now. The two fields will look much the same, but any lines that have a link in them will certainly be on a line of their own.

8. Add a line to filter the list, as it stands, to reduce it so that it shows only the lines with links in them:

```
filter pPageSource with "*a href*/a>"
```

9. The * characters are wildcards that reduces the list so that it only contains the lines that have both `a href` and `/a>`. Try the button again.

10. Now you'll see that there are only lines with links in them, but they still include the junk either side of the link itself. The part we need is between the first and second quote marks, and using the `itemdelimiter`, we can get at that bit. Add the following lines:

```
set the itemdelimiter to quote
  repeat with a = 1 to the number of lines in pPageSource
    put item 2 of line a of pPageSource into line a of pPageSource
  end repeat
```

11. When you now click on the button, you should get a list of only the URL part of each line. However note that most of the links start with / and not `http`.

12. Make another function in the stack script that will change the links to full path:

```
function getPath pPageURL,pLinkURL
end getPath
```

13. Now, add the code needed to cope with the variations of URL (to function `getPath`), starting with it's full path:

```
if pLinkURL contains "://" then
  return pLinkURL
end if
```

14. If you recall from earlier, we saved the URL of the main page in a global variable, `gPageURL`. For the case where the link is a root relative (it starts with a /), we want to combine the host location and the link URL:

```
set the itemdelimiter to "/"
if char 1 of pLinkURL is "/" then
  return item 1 to 3 of pPageURL & pLinkURL
else
```

15. When that first character is not /, it may start with `../` to step up one level in the server structure. Deleting the last part of the page URL will give us what we need to combine with the link URL:

```
if char 1 to 3 of pLinkURL is "../" then
  delete the last item of pPageURL
  delete the last item of pPageURL
  delete char 1 to 2 of pLinkURL
  return pPageURL & pLinkURL
else
For other cases we combine the page URL and the link URL:
  delete the last item of pPageURL
  return pPageURL & "/" & pLinkURL
  end if
end if
```

16. Lastly, if all of these checks fail, we will return an empty string, so that this strange structured link URL doesn't go on to confuse us later:

```
    return ""
end getPath
```

17. To get the `getLinks` function to use the `getPath` function, we need to make a change to the script shown in step 9:

```
    repeat with a = 1 to the number of lines in pPageSource
    put getPath(gPageURL,item 2 of line a of pPageSource) into line
a of pPageSource
    end repeat
```

What just happened?

In stages, we developed a function that can find the links in a web page's source text ending with a set of full path URLs that we can present to the user.

The missing links

The one missing piece in the test stack is the global variable that stores the page URL. In the case of the app stack, the value is provided by the browser control's `browserFinishedLoading` function, but here, we need to plug in a value for testing purposes.

Place a global declaration line in the button's script and the stack script. In the button script, fill in the variable with our test case value. The script will then be like this:

```
global gPageURL

on mouseUp
  put "http://www.runrev.com/" into gPageURL
  put url gPageURL into field 1
  put getLinks(field 1) into field 2
end mouseUp
```

Try the button now, you should see a list of full path URLs in your second field. If it works correctly, copy the two stack functions and the global declaration line and paste them into the stack script of the WebScraper stack.

One more thing...

The tab bar script includes an init line. This will call the card script; in this case, the Links card script, but it doesn't exist yet! Let's make it.

Time for action – adding the links card's init handler

Before proceeding, make sure that you are happy with the functions in the test stack and that you have copied them to the WebScraper stack script using the following steps:

1. Go to the Links card of the WebScraper stack.

2. Edit the card script and add these global variables and `init` function:

```
global gPageHTML, gLinks

on init
if the platform is "iphone" or the platform is "android" then
  put getLinks(gPageHTML) into gLinks
  if the number of lines in gLinks = 0 then
    answer "There are no links in this page!"
  else
    mobilePick gLinks, 0
    if the result > 0 then
     put the result into tLinkLine
     put line tLinkLine of gLinks into tLink
     go card "Browser"
     set the mgText of group "url" to tLink
     set the Text of field "NavBar" to "Browser"
     mobileControlSet "Page", "url", the mgText of group "url"
     end if
    end if
  end if
end init
```

3. Do a Test of the app.

4. In the iPhone Simulator or Android device, if that's what you're using, change the URL to `http://www.runrev.com/` and select the **Go** button.

5. When the page is loaded, select the **Links** tab button.

6. You should now be looking at the list of links from the RunRev page; only this time, it's presented in a native picker list.

7. Select a link from the list and then **Done**.

8. You will be taken back to the Browser card with the linked page loaded.

What just happened?

The card script we entered does the same job as the button in the test stack; in that, it calls to the stack functions to get a list of links. Here, rather than putting the list into a plain field, we used LiveCode's ability to open a native picker control using the line:

```
mobilePick gLinks,1
```

The required parameters of this function are a list of items to be shown and an index position to be the one that is selected. By entering 1, the first item is selected by default. The result that comes back from the picker is an index of the item that was selected, and we can use this to look up the matching line in the gLinks variable.

The remaining lines take us back to the Browser card, set the URL to be loaded, and also change the NavBar to reflect the card name.

The Text card

Making the Text card work is a lot simpler, but includes an unbelievably complex regular expression line, which can be found at:

```
http://stackoverflow.com/questions/3951485/regex-extracting-readable-
non-code-text-and-urls-from-html-documents
```

Time for action – setting up the Text card

We will start off in the test stack that you made, so that we can get the function working there before adding it to the WebScraper stack.

1. Duplicate the button you made when extracting links. Change the function call getLinks to getText; the rest of the script can remain the same.

2. Edit the script of the test stack and add this function:

```
function getText pPageSource
  put replaceText(pPageSource,"(?:<(?P<tag>script|style)
[\s\S]*?</(?P=tag)>)|(?:<!--[\s\S]*?-->)|(?:<[\s\S]*?>)","") into
pPageSource
  replace lf with "" in pPageSource
  replace tab with " " in pPageSource
  return pPageSource
end getText
```

3. Try clicking on the button you just made. You should see your second field filled with just the text parts of the web page.

4. Copy the function and go back to the WebScraper stack script. Paste the function there.

5. Go to the Text card of the stack and from the MobGUI window, drag the **Multiline Text** control onto the card. Set its name to `PageText`.

6. Resize the control to fill the area between the NavBar and the Tab-bar. You may have to use the LiveCode Inspector to modify the size if the text does not fill the field.

7. In the MobGUI window properties for the control, uncheck the box for **Editable**.

8. Edit the card script and add this `init` function:

```
global gPageHTML

on init
  if the platform is "iphone" or the platform is "android" then
    mobileControlSet "PageText","text",getText(gPageHTML)
  end if
end init
```

9. Try a **Test** of the app.

10. In the **Browser** card, change the URL from `http://google.com/` to `http://runrev.com/` and click on **Go**.

11. Press the **Text** tab button at the bottom.

12. You should now be on the **Text** card and should be able to see the text elements from the web page displayed in a native scrolling text field.

What just happened?

This enormously long regular expression ran through the web page source and removed anything that was script, style, or just tag information, leaving the text parts alone. However, it would leave it with lots of spare line feed characters and tab characters, which we went on to remove using the LiveCode `replace` function. The final text may not be perfect, but you can use the standard mobile text features to copy parts of the text for use in other apps.

The Media card

The Media card is going to start off very much like the Links card, with an `init` function in the card script and a stack script function to extract the media links from the page.

Time for action – extracting a list of media links

There probably is a regular expression that would extract all the `src` links from a page, but we're only interested in things that we know LiveCode is able to show or play. So in these steps, we'll use a more devious way to extract just the links we can handle:

1. You may as well head over to the test stack!

2. Make a third button by duplicating one of the other two and change the `getLinks` or `getText` part in the button script to call `getMedia` instead.

3. In the stack script, enter all of this:

```
global gPageURL

function getMedia pPageSource
   put ".jpg,.png,.gif,.jpeg,.mov,.mp4,m4v,.mp3" into tExtensions
   repeat with a = 1 to the number of items in tExtensions
     put item a of tExtensions into tExtension
     replace tExtension with tExtension & "*" & return in
pPageSource
   end repeat
   repeat with a = the number of lines in pPageSource down to 1
     put line a of pPageSource into tLine
     if the last char of tLine is "*" then
       delete the last char of tLine
       put removeLeaders(gPageURL,tLine) into line a of pPageSource
     else
       delete line a of pPageSource
     end if
   end repeat
   return pPageSource
end getMedia

function removeLeaders pPageURL,pLinkURL
   put quote&"'()" into tDelimiters
   repeat with a = 1 to the number of chars in tDelimiters
     put char a of tDelimiters into tDelimiter
     set the itemdelimiter to tDelimiter
     put the last item of pLinkURL into pLinkURL
   end repeat
   return getPath(pPageURL,pLinkURL)
end removeLeaders
```

4. Click on the button and you should see a list of full paths to the various images in the web page.

What just happened?

This devious approach involved the task of finding any place where the media of interest is mentioned and adding an asterisk and return character in order to make sure that the link was easily identified and at the end of a unique line. Then, each of these lines were sent to another function, `removeLeaders`, to remove any other text that was earlier in the line than at the start of the link. Finally, the same `getPath` function we used while extracting links was used to give us full paths to the media files.

Now that we have a list of media links, we need to add the card level handlers required to present the list to the user and to load their selected media item onto the card window.

Time for action – setting up the Media card scripts

Copy the functions that you have proved to work, in the test stack script and paste them into the WebScraper stack script. Then, perform these steps:

1. Go to the Media card. As with the Links card, we're not going to add any controls to the card, as we'll do that with the script. So, edit the card script.

2. Here's the Media card's `init` function and the needed global variables:

```
global gPageHTML,gMediaList

on init
  if the platform is "iphone" or the platform is "android" then
    put getMedia(gPageHTML) into gMediaList
    if the number of lines in gMediaList = 0 then
      answer "There is no media in this page!"
    else
      set the itemdelimiter to "/"
      put empty into tMediaNames
      repeat with a = 1 to the number of lines in gMediaList
        put the last item of line a of gMediaList into line a of
tMediaNames
      end repeat
      mobilePick tMediaNames,1
      if the result > 0 then
        put the result into tMediaLine
        showMedia line tMediaLine of gMediaList
      end if
    end if
  end if
end init
```

3. Unlike the Links case, we've built up a list of just the filename part of the URL, to be seen in a native picker, and when we've selected something we will call a showMedia function in the stack script.

4. Edit the stack script.

5. Create the showMedia function:

```
on showMedia pMediaFile
   if there is an image "mediaImage" then delete image "mediaImage"
   set the itemdelimiter to "."
   switch (the last item of pMediaFile)
     case "png"
     case "gif"
     case "jpg"
     case "jpeg"
       new image
       set the name of image the number of images to "mediaImage"
       set the filename of image "mediaImage" to pMediaFile
       break
     case "mp4"
     case "m4v"
     case "mov"
     case "mp3"
       set the showController of the templatePlayer to true
       play video pMediaFile
       break
   end switch
end showMedia
```

6. Test the app.

7. You can start with the google.com page; click on the **Media** tab button to see a list of the images used on that page.

8. Select an image from the list and click on **Done**.

9. The image should appear on the card.

10. Go back to the **Browser** card and change the URL to http://www.apple.com/.

11. Apple usually includes some video link thumbnails on the main page. click on one of those, so that you see the large video player. However, don't play it!

12. Click on the **Media** tab button to see a list of all the media on that page.

13. Scroll down the list and look for one of the longer-named items that seems like it must be a video.

14. Select that item and press **Done**. The video should load and play on the card.

15. Use the video controller's **Done** button when you are finished watching the video to return to the **Media** card.

16. You can then click on the **Media** tab button again to make the picker reappear.

17. Go back to the **Browser** card and enter a URL that contains examples of MP3 files. `http://www.ntonyx.com/mp3_songs.htm` is one such example.

18. Click on the **Media** tab button to return to the **Media** card with the list of all the media on that page, which in this case will be mainly MP3 files.

19. Select one of the MP3s from the list and click on **Done**. The MP3 should play in the same player that the video is played in.

What just happened?

In this example, we made use of both a standard LiveCode control, the image, and also a native control, the video player. LiveCode handles the setting up of the player and with the very simple "play video videoname" syntax, we were able to invoke the native player. It was able to play both video and audio files.

The Keepers card

Actually, this should be the Keepers *cards*. These cards are where you can stash media that you've found interesting. For file size reasons, we're actually just going to store the URL to the media; after all, a long video would soon use up your device's storage!

Time for action – setting up the Keepers card

1. Go to the **Keepers** card and create a MobGUI button for **Prev**, **Next**, and **Play Media**. Make a MobGUI **Multiline** field and name it `mediaURL`. Be sure to uncheck the **Auto delete** option, so that it keeps the URL data when we change cards. Also uncheck the **Editable** option. You should now have something looking like the following screenshot:

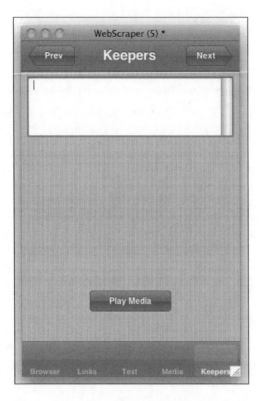

2. Add these lines to the `mouseUp` handler of the **Prev** button:

```
if the number of this card is > 5 then
   go previous
end if
```

3. Add these lines to the `mouseUp` handler of the **Next** button. Note that `- 1` is used since the last card is the MobGUI card:

```
if the number of this card < the number of cards - 1 then
   go next
end if
```

4. Add this line to the Play Media button's `mouseUp` handler:

```
showMedia the mgText of group "mediaURL"
```

5. Select the four controls and Group them. Check the box that says **Behave like a background**. Name the group `keeperbuttons`.

6. Edit the script of the new group. Add this `refresh` handler:

```
on refresh
  set the itemdelimiter to "."
  if char 1 of the last item of the mgText of group "mediaURL" is
"m" then
    show group "Play Media"
  else
    hide group "Play Media"
    showMedia the mgText of group "mediaURL"
  end if
end refresh
```

7. We need to go back and add things to the **Media** card.

8. Go to the **Media** card and add a MobGUI button. Set the name and label to `Keep Media`.

9. One tricky thing is that media will play full screen on smaller screens and by the time you see the **Keep Media** button, the video has already gone away. We can work around this by storing the URL of the last shown media in a global variable.

10. In the **Media** card script, change the `init` function, so that the later lines read like this:

```
if the result > 0 then
  put the result into tMediaLine
  put line tMediaLine of gMediaList into gLastMedia
  showMedia gLastMedia
end if
```

11. Change the global variable declaration line to include the `gLastMedia` variable.

12. Set the `mouseUp` handler of the **Keep Media** button to be this:

```
on mouseUp
  global gLastMedia
  go  card (the number of cards -1)
  if the mgText of group "mediaURL" is not empty then
  new card
  end if
```

```
      set the mgText of group "mediaURL" to gLastMedia
      save stack "WebScaper" as (specialFolderPath("documents") & "/
WebScraper.livecode")
      send "refresh" to group "keeperButtons"
   end mouseUp
```

13. Now, only one last step is required for the stack to save the media. We need to create a launcher app like we did earlier in this chapter. Create a stack named LaunchScraper with the following stack script:

```
on openStack
   set the defaultFolder to specialFolderPath("Documents")
   if there is not a file "WebScraper.livecode" then
     put the filename of this stack into masterfile
     set the itemdelimiter to "/"
     put "WebScraper.livecode" into the last item of masterfile
     put specialFolderPath("engine") & "/WebScraper.livecode" into
masterfile
     put specialFolderPath("Documents") & "/WebScraper.livecode"
into appfile
     put URL ("binfile:" & masterfile) into URL ("binfile:" &
appfile)
   end if
   go stack specialFolderPath("Documents") & "/WebScraper.livecode"
   answer the filename of this stack
end openStack
```

14. Make sure that the Launch Scraper and Web Scraper apps are in the same folder. Open only the Launch Scraper app and make sure that the Web Scraper app is included in the **Copy files** of the **Standalone Application Settings**.

15. Select your **Test Target** device and then **Test**. Note that the last answer statement will display the path and the filename where the main app is stored on your device. This can be commented out once you are comfortable that it is working.

16. Use the **Browser** card to load a page with plenty of images, videos, or sounds on it and go to the **Media** card to see those listed.

17. Select any item followed by a click on **Done**.

18. If you like the image, sound, or video, use the **Keep Media** button to go to the end of the stack to save the media's URL.

19. Choose more bits of media and keep them.

20. Go to the **Keepers** section and use the **Next** and **Prev** buttons to browse through the items you've kept.

21. The images should appear automatically and the video and audio can be started with the **Play Media** button.

What just happened?

We added the last feature of our application, a set of cards where we can go to view the bits of media that we've chosen to keep.

Have a go hero – add some preset locations

If you do make the Web Scraper app and start to find it useful, it's quite likely that there will be a set of web pages that you'd like to go back to again and again. To type the URL every time would be tedious. So, why not make a hidden field on the **Browser** card and type in a list of your favorite pages. Add a button to the card too, which will bring up a list of those pages for you to choose from. The one you choose can then load the **Browser** control at the desired page. All of the steps to do this were covered in the *The Links card* section.

It's pretty certain that if you've carefully followed all the steps in this chapter and indeed all the steps were perfect, you still wouldn't have an app ready to be submitted to the app stores! You would require a splash screen, a main menu, icons on the tab buttons as well and some love from a graphic designer! Feature wise, it would be nice if the images you keep could be zoomed and panned.

Summary

Some of the topics that we covered here are less glamorous, mostly the ones about processing HTML text, but we did also use a few mobile features. We demonstrated how a native app can store data for subsequent usage, and how to make and control a web browser. The use of a native picker to present lists was covered. We also created a native scrolling field that had all the normal OS-specific abilities and played video and audio using the native media players.

The next chapter is almost entirely about dealing with graphics, so we'll make sure to use some image manipulating gestures and you could revisit the Web Scraper app later to add the same features to the Keepers cards.

5

Making a Jigsaw Puzzle Application

Picture this...

So far, we've been dealing with a lot of text or calling mobile OS features. These are neat things, but they're not that visual. If you were longing to mess around with pictures and image data, your time has come!

LiveCode isn't naturally a graphics powerhouse and its way of handling image data (often referred to as "bitmap data" by other tools) is somewhat unusual. It effectively stores the pixels of an image as a series of single byte characters to represent the red, green, and blue values of each pixel. Handling a final image is quite flexible, but in order to create something along the lines of a jigsaw puzzle, we need to understand the format of `imageData`, a LiveCode property.

In this chapter, we will:

◆ Examine the way LiveCode stores bitmap data in an image object

◆ Find a way to use a single bitmap in place of 50 buttons

◆ Make a collision detection map

◆ Create a jigsaw puzzle app that takes advantage of several mobile device features

Image data format

In other authoring tools, such as Adobe Director and Adobe Flash, bitmap data is stored as a matrix of 24-bit or 32-bit values. If you want to know the color of the 20th pixel from the left edge in the 15th row from the top of the image, you would have to use a `getPixel` function with these numbers filled in. In Flash, which uses a zero starting point for all its variable types, you would have to write the following code:

```
pixelcolor = bitmapvariable.getPixel(19,14);
```

You would in fact have to start this line with `var pixelcolor:uint`, but here we're looking at the main differences and not the oddities of having a strongly typed programming language! In Director, which like LiveCode uses 1 based variables, you would have to write the following code:

```
pixelcolor = imagevariable.getPixel(20,15)
```

Again, there's no need for variable typing or even a semicolon at the end of the line. While we digress, Flash too, doesn't need the semicolon at the end or at least, you don't have to type it yourself. Flash knew what you meant! Getting back to the point...

In LiveCode, each pixel of an image is represented by four bytes, which you can access as if they are single-byte characters. The range of values in a byte is 0-255, and storing such values, especially the value `0`, in character variables does not work out well. Therefore, you would have to convert the character value into a numeric value before making use of it. The basic problem is that, although the numeric value is stored in a variable, when you come to do calculations on it, LiveCode wants to work in Base 10 arithmetic and not in the binary form inside the variable. You have to convert the variable into something that can be processed using the `charToNum` function.

So, why would a character variable not like zeros you ask! Well, in the earliest days of personal computers, the predominant programming language was Pascal. In Pascal, a variable that contained a literal string needed a way to know how long the string was. The first byte of a Pascal string stores the length of the string, which was fine up to 255 characters, and in those days, it was most likely thought of as enough, and more than anyone would ever need! In real life though, strings can be longer than 255 characters. This paragraph alone is over 900 characters long. To solve this issue, the C programming language used a zero to indicate the end of a *C String*. You could have a million characters in a row; however, only the last one would be a zero. RGB values don't care about the limitations of C strings and there are zeros all over the place, which is why we convert it to a numeric value as soon as we can.

In addition to the oddity of each pixel being stored as four bytes of information, there's also no way to tell specify rows and columns. All the pixels in an image have their four bytes end to end; you have to do a calculation to know where in the data the pixel you're looking for is located. If you have worked on a bitmap editor before, say Photoshop or Gimp, you must be aware that you select content based on an *X* and *Y* co-ordinate value that correspond to the column and row that the pixel is located in. LiveCode doesn't let you access bitmaps in this way. Hence, we need to do a calculation.

Here's how the pixel from the preceding example would be retrieved in LiveCode if you want it as a 24-bit value:

```
put getPixel(""test image"",20,15) into pixelcolor

function getPixel pImage,pX,pY
  put the imageData of image pImage into tImageData
  put the width of image pImage into tWidth
  put ((pY-1)*tWidth + (pX-1)) * 4 into tStartChar
  put charToNum(char tStartChar+2 of tImageData) into tRed
  put charToNum(char tStartChar+3 of tImageData) into tGreen
  put charToNum(char tStartChar+4 of tImageData) into tBlue
  return tRed*65536+tGreen*256+tBlue
end getPixel
```

On the face of it, this is one of the few cases where the way it's done in LiveCode is considerably longer than in other languages. However, quite often, you really need the red, green, and blue values from the pixel, and in other languages, you have to take extra steps to extract these values.

The extra steps needed to make the returned number a 24-bit RGB value are no big deal, as LiveCode is easily extended by your own functions. If you need the 24-bit value, use the preceding function and you will have added a `getPixel` function to the LiveCode language. You still have to do the calculations to even get at just the red value. Maybe one day, LiveCode will have a built-in `getPixel` function that works quicker than your own function. The 24-bit number returned here is in fact represented as three decimal numbers and not as a 24-bit binary value, but it would still be generally referred to as *24 bit*.

Mystery byte...

The first character of the four that represent one pixel is not used. LiveCode has tutorials on how to use `imageData`, where that byte is referred to as Alpha. That makes sense, as even the other tools that give you a 32-bit number have the value broken up into Alpha, Red, Green, and Blue. Why doesn't that byte, which RunRev calls Alpha, contain the alpha value? Who knows!

One possibility is that the value doesn't serve its purpose well enough. When talking about alpha transparency, you sometimes may mean that the image is transparent, as might be the case in a GIF image. Other times, you may mean that it's translucent, where it's only partially see-through.

To solve the ambiguous nature of the problem, LiveCode has two other properties of an image, `maskData` and `alphaData`:

```
put the maskData of image "test image" into tMaskData
put the alphaData of image "test image" into tAlphaData
```

These properties of an image still have all the rows end to end, and you have to do the calculation to find where a given pixel's alpha value is stored.

With `maskData`, you get a set of values for each of the pixels. For every value other than 0, the pixel is visible.

With `alphaData`, you get a set of values of the opaqueness of the pixel. 0 would be fully transparent, 255 would be fully opaque, and the values in between will be translucent. 128 would be 50 percent opaque.

Later in this chapter, we are going to make use of both `maskData` and `alphaData`, and we will refer to the 0-255 `alphaData` value as its *transparency*, and the zero or nonzero `maskData` value as its *mask*.

Misusing imageData

The topics in the LiveCode online tutorials include manipulation of `imageData`, turning a colored image into a grayscale one (this particular example of turning a colored image is located at `http://lessons.runrev.com/s/lessons/m/4071/l/25371-vision-how-do-i-convert-a-color-image-to-grayscale`). We're not going to do that here. Instead, we'll use the values in the image, mask, and alpha to achieve some neat things that don't change the image at all. In fact, in some cases, we won't even see the image!

Time for action – testing a getPixel function

Before getting to useful examples, let's make a `getPixel` function to obtain the color components of a point in the image and then complete a quick test case. The following steps will help you in this process:

1. Make a new Mainstack. Click on **Save** to save it as **ImageDataTests**.

 We'll use the same stack to illustrate several things and at the end, we may dare to try it on a mobile device!

2. Set the stack's resolution to the size of your largest test device or just try 1024 x 768 if you'll be using the iPad Simulator.

3. From the **File** menu, navigate to **Import as Control | Image** and select any small image file you have, to place it in the upper-left corner of the card window. The next example, uses a LiveCode logo image that can easily be obtained from any LiveCode web page.

4. Place a new `Graphic` object next to the image. It's going to show a single color, so just make it big enough so that you can easily see the color. Name it `swatch`.

5. Set graphics to default to show an empty box, so type this in the message box to fill it:

```
set the filled of graphic 1 to true
```

6. Edit the script of the image and type these lines in:

```
on mouseMove pMx,pMy
  --put getPixel(the short name of me,pMx - the left of me,pMy -
the top of me) into tPixelColor
  --set the backgroundColor of graphic "swatch" to tPixelColor
end mouseMove
```

7. Note that the two lines are commented out. LiveCode would only complain if we keep asking for `getPixel` before we create that function!

8. Edit the stack script. Add the `getPixel` function, which is very much like the one shown in the Image data format we discussed in the preceding steps:

```
function getPixel pImage,pX,pY
   put the imageData of image pImage into tImageData
   put the width of image pImage into tWidth
   put ((pY-1)*tWidth + (pX-1)) * 4 into tStartChar
   put charToNum(char tStartChar+2 of tImageData) into tRed
   put charToNum(char tStartChar+3 of tImageData) into tGreen
   put charToNum(char tStartChar+4 of tImageData) into tBlue
   return tRed,tGreen,tBlue
end getPixel
```

9. Back in the image script, uncomment the two lines. Start pointing at the image and you should see the swatch graphic change color to match the pixel under the cursor.

What just happened?

We made a very simple example case of how to use the color of a pixel in an image; in this case, how to colorize a swatch. As setting `backgroundColor` of a graphic requires `redvalue`, `greenvalue`, and `bluevalue`, we didn't need to convert the values from the image to a 24-bit number and the `getPixel` function was able to return `tRed,tGreen,tBlue`.

Now, there isn't really any advantage to the way we did that compared to the built-in `mouseColor` function. However, at least we gave the `getPixel` function a tryout!

Pop quiz – how many bits in a byte?

Bytes was mentioned a few times in this chapter and you may well know about *bit depth* as we've talked about digital photographs. So tell me, how many bits are there in a byte?

1. 32
2. 24
3. 8
4. Depends on how hungry you are

Answer: 8

We won't even talk about bits or bytes in the rest of this chapter; however, if only for the interest to mathematicians, it's good to know that a byte is 8 bits. A bit is a binary digit, and when you start to think of bits in those terms, you will see that a byte can store 2 to the power of 8 values in it (binary being Base 2). This comes into play when you look at the length of a Pascal string (2 to the power of 8 is 256, hence the range of characters in a Pascal String is 0-255) and it helps you realize that if a picture is made up of one byte, for each pixel's red, green, and blue values, it's a 24-bit picture. Once you add in another byte of data for the alpha channel, you have a 32-bit picture.

Simulating lots of buttons

In some applications, you need to know exactly which area of an image the user is pointing at. For example, when there is a map and you want to show information related to the region the user has clicked on, this could be done using a lot of rectangular buttons or you could break the regions into graphics and use a `mouseEnter` handler to detect which region it is. Instead, you could use a single image to represent all the regions.

Time for action – making a map of the United States

There are plenty of places online to get public domain images to use in your applications. Search for `public domain images` and you will see links to Wikipedia articles, government sites, and other sites that let you download images that are free to use. The map shown in the following steps came from the file at:

`http://upload.wikimedia.org/wikipedia/commons/3/32/Blank_US_Map.svg`.

1. Make a new field named `states`. Find an alphabetical list of the 50 united states to paste it into the field or you can type them in!

2. Make another field, set the text size to 24, and the size of the field wide enough for *New Hampshire* to fit in (just the words, not the entire state!). Name the field `state`.

Download the completed map

Note that you can save a lot of work here by downloading the `us-map.png` file from the support file section for this book, which you can find at `www.PacktPub.com`.

3. If you have Adobe Illustrator, open the SVG file with it. If not, open it with GIMP. Pixelmator is a low-cost alternative on Macintosh OS X.

4. In alphabetical order, fill in each state with a color where the red, green, and blue values match the line number of that state + 100 . We're adding 100 so that the shades of gray we'll see will not be so dark.

5. Continue the same through all the states. Here's how it will start to look like in Illustrator, where Idaho is about to be colored as 112, 112, 112:

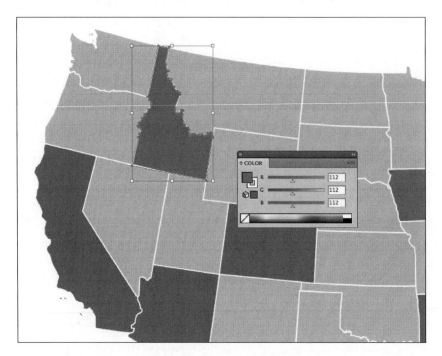

6. Change the size of the map, so that it would fill about a third of the stack window, and choose **Export**.

Color profile settings

LiveCode treats bitmaps in a way that ignores color profile information in the image, and that would ruin this thing we're trying to do. While exporting an image, check whether there is an option to set the color profile to genericRGB. If there isn't, then use a utility such as Color Sync to apply the genericRGB color profile. Once the image is saved, there is something you can do to make sure that it gets imported into LiveCode OK. Before importing, set the screen gamma to 2.23 by typing in the message box and press *Enter*. This will set LiveCode to the right settings to make sure that the color values appear correctly.

7. If you're using Illustrator, set the background to be **White** and anti-aliasing to be **None**. With GIMP, make sure that the PNG is saved without an alpha channel.

8. Type this line followed by the *Enter* key into the message box:

```
set the screengamma to 2.23
```

9. Import the PNG into your `ImageDataTests` stack.

10. Set the image's script to this:

```
on mouseMove pMx,pMy
  put getPixel(the short name of me,pMx - the left of me,pMy - the
top of me) into tStateColor
  set the itemdelimiter to comma
  put item 1 of tStateColor - 100 into tLine
  put line tLine of field "states" into field "state"
end mouseMove
```

11. Try pointing at the different states, at least point at the ones that you have colored. The state name should appear in the `state` field.

What just happened?

For this case, we only needed to look at the value of the red channel for the pixel under the cursor (the green and blue values are the same because we used a gray color value for both). Rather than writing another function to get only the red part of the data, we reused the existing `getPixel` function, but then only took notice of the first item that the function returned. That number, after subtracting 100 that we had added to it to make the shades not be so dark, was then used as a lookup value to get the corresponding state name.

Pop quiz – getting the big picture

The example map image was an SVG file. Is an SVG file smaller than a PNG file for a given image? (do a little Wikipedia research and decide on the answer.)

1. Yes

2. No

3. Depends on the nature of the image

Answer: 3

SVG is a description of how to draw the image, whereas PNG is a description of the pixels in the image. In PNG, this information is also data compressed in a lossless way. For the example map, at its original size, a 24-bit PNG is half the size of the SVG file. There is a lot of data needed to describe the outlines of the U.S. states! If the image needs to be enlarged, the PNG would become a bigger-sized file and the SVG would remain at the same file size. On the other hand, if an image was a rectangle piece of a diagonal gradient, the SVG would be tiny and the PNG would be huge because there are no long runs of the same-colored pixels for the data compression to work well.

Using maskData for collision detection

In old 2D maze adventure games, your character would move in distinct chunks, and while checking whether there was a wall or gap, the program only had to check relatively few locations. The occupied spots could be stored in an array, taking up little memory.

With other maze games, like those of marble maze tilt boards, you have to detect collisions at a much finer degree. A full-blown physics engine could take care of the problem, but it's possible to get some interesting results by storing the maze as an image and checking the pixels that are in front of your character or marble as the case may be.

In a full-featured game, it would be better to use `imageData` or perhaps `alphaData`, so that you can tell when you are going to hit something, and from the value you read, you can also tell what it is you have hit. In the marble maze game, you need to know when you have gone over a hole, for example.

For this next test though, we'll just use `maskData` and see what we can do about not hitting the thing that is in front of us.

Time for action – making a racecourse

We're going to make a racecourse for little cars to move around. We'll make it out of the stack we've built! First, we need to convert what is on the card into an image that represents walls and spaces:

1. Using the LiveCode draw tools, add a bunch of objects to the `ImageDataTest` stack. These are going to be the obstacles in the racecourse.

2. To create the image we'll need, type this in the message box:

   ```
   import snapshot from rect the rect of this stack
   ```

3. The preceding command will take a screenshot of the card window and place it onto the card as a new *image* control. The new image will overlay the whole card, so will not be noticeable. You can confirm that the image was created and select it with the Project Browser.

4. Right-click on the image that was created and select **Launch Editor**. This will open the image in the bitmap editor that you have set in **Preferences/General**. You will be prompted by LiveCode to select an editor if you haven't previously done so.

5. In your image editor's **Layers** window, duplicate the initial single layer.

6. Make a new layer that is transparent beneath the duplicate image layer.

7. Delete the original layer.

8. Use the editor's *Magic Wand* to select the white space of the card image in the layer with the image in it (not the transparent layer). Delete the selected area to reveal the transparent layer.

9. Inverse the selection and fill it with a dark color (the color doesn't matter, as it's used just so we can see where the holes are).

10. Take some time to fill in any small gaps. Also, place a thick border around the outside of the image. This shows how the card looks like and how the snapshot image should look like by now:

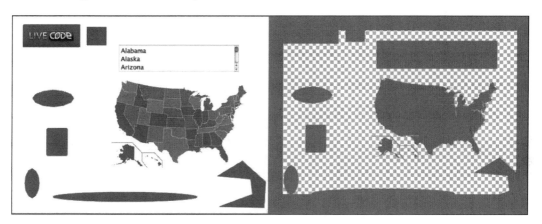

11. **Merge** the layers of the document and then select **Save**.

12. Return to LiveCode and click on the **Update** button, and the snapshot image will be updated to reflect the changes you've made.

13. Give the image the name `backdrop`. Later, we'll set the image behind other objects, but for now, we'll leave it on top of everything else.

What just happened?

We just made a pretty strange looking racecourse! In a real top-down racing game, you would have to carefully design a nice-looking racecourse and make a duplicate of the image for collision detection. In the duplicate, you would have to erase the parts of the image that represent where cars are allowed to drive and then, you would have to fill the rest of the image with a flat color. Players would see the nice-looking racecourse, and underneath that would be the duplicate flat color version used to detect collisions.

We now need a car that drives itself around the course we've made.

Time for action – making a racecar

Take as much time as you would like to create an image of the car. Make it so that it faces right. Then, once it's in the stack, we'll start adding the required functions to its script. A size of about 40 pixels across should be about right. Our sample car is also available on www. PacktPub.com. The following is a close-up image of what we're talking about, as seen in Photoshop:

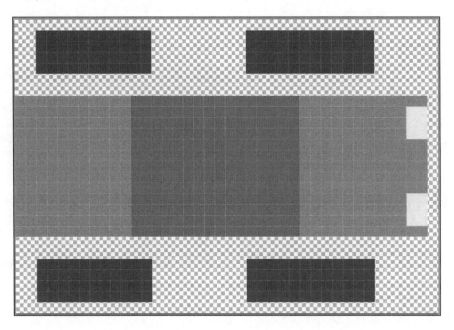

Yours can be even better than that, if you like! Save it as a 24-bit PNG that has transparency. Ok, start your engines…:

1. Import the image as a control and place it somewhere in the white area of the `ImageDataTests` stack. Name it `car1`.

2. Duplicate the image as many times as you like (the following script can handle up to 100 cars) and name each one as a sequence, `car2`, `car3`, and so on.

3. Arguably, the correct *object-oriented* way to proceed would be to place some functions on the images and some in the card or stack script, but for performance reasons, we'll put everything in the stack script. Open the stack script.

4. Add a line for the global variables we'll need:

```
global gBackdropMaskData,gMaskWidth,gSpeeds,gMovingCars,gMaskWidth
```

5. We'll add a Start/Stop button soon, which will call a function to toggle whether the cars are moving or not. Add the toggle function to the stack script:

```
on startStopCars
  if gMovingCars is true then
    put false into gMovingCars
  else
    put the maskData of image "backdrop" into gBackdropMaskData
    put the width of image "backdrop" into gMaskWidth
    setSpeeds
    put true into gMovingCars
    send moveCars to this card in 2 ticks
  end if
end startStopCars
```

6. The `setSpeeds` handler, which is called by `startStopCars`, will initialize the `gSpeeds` variable with a random speed for each of the car images. It will also set the initial direction to zero as well as position the car at a known location in the white area (`200, 200` in this case). Add the `setSpeeds` handler to the stack script below the `startStopCars` handler:

```
on setSpeeds
  put empty into gSpeeds
  repeat with a = 1 to 100
    put "car" & a into carname
    if there is a image carname then
      put (random(10)+10)/10 into item 1 of line a of gSpeeds
      put 0 into item 2 of line a of gSpeeds
```

```
        set the loc of image carname to 200,200
     else
       exit repeat
     end if
  end repeat
end setSpeeds
```

7. In the `moveCars` handler, shown in step 8, we're going to look at the `gBackdropMaskData` variable to check whether the car is going to run into something solid. Add this `hitBarrier` function:

```
function hitBarrier pX,pY
  put (pY-1)*gMaskWidth + pX into tStartChar
  put charToNum(char tStartChar of gBackdropMaskData) into
tMaskValue
  if tMaskValue = 255 then return true
  else return false
end hitBarrier
```

8. The `moveCars` handler is initially called by the `startStopCars` handler, and then, it calls itself after every two ticks until the `gMovingCars` variable is set to `false`. Type in the long `moveCars` handler into the stack script:

```
on moveCars
  put the long time
  lock screen
  repeat with a = 1 to 100
    put "car" & a into carname
    put .1 into anglechange
    if there is a image carname then
      put 0 into counter
      repeat while counter < 20
        add 1 to counter
        put item 1 of line a of gSpeeds into tCarSpeed
        put item 2 of line a of gSpeeds into tCarDirection
        put item 1 of the loc of image carname into tCarX
        put item 2 of the loc of image carname into tCarY
        put the round of ((cos(tCarDirection)*tCarSpeed)*20 +
tCarX) into tLookAheadX
        put the round of ((sin(tCarDirection)*tCarSpeed)*20 +
tCarY) into tLookAheadY
        if hitBarrier(tLookAheadX,tLookAheadY) then
          put tCarDirection + anglechange into item 2 of line a of
gSpeeds
```

```
        put anglechange * -1 * ((20 - random(10))/10) into
anglechange
        put max(1,tCarSpeed - .1) into item 1 of line a of
gSpeeds
      else
        put min(3,tCarSpeed + .05) into item 1 of line a of
gSpeeds
        exit repeat
      end if
      end repeat
    set the loc of image carname to item 1 of the loc of image
carname + (tLookAheadX-item 1 of the loc of image carname)/10,item
2 of the loc of image carname + (tLookAheadY-item 2 of the loc of
image carname)/10
    set the angle of image carname to 360 - item 2 of line a of
gSpeeds / PI * 180
    else
      exit repeat
    end if
  end repeat
  unlock screen
  if gMovingCars is true then send moveCars to this card in 2
ticks
end moveCars
```

Collision avoidance

Take a moment to look at the moveCars handler; what is it doing? You will no doubt have heard about collision detection; this is where you have code that recognizes when one object has collided with another object or a wall perhaps. You might as well trigger an explosion or a collision sound when that happens. For our example though, we actually don't want things to collide, as we want the cars to turn before they collide. For each car, up to 100 of them, we will look ahead of the car to check whether it collides with the edges of the course. If it's going to do so, we will change the direction that the car is heading toward, repeatedly, until a safe forward direction is found.

9. Add a Start/Stop Cars button to the card window and set its script as:

```
on mouseUp
  startStopCars
end mouseUp
```

10. Select the backdrop image and choose **Send to Back** from the **Object** menu.

11. It's a good idea to save it now!

12. Click on the Run/Browse tool and then on the Start/Stop Cars button to see your cars drive around the interface. Here's how it looks like when 20 cars move about:

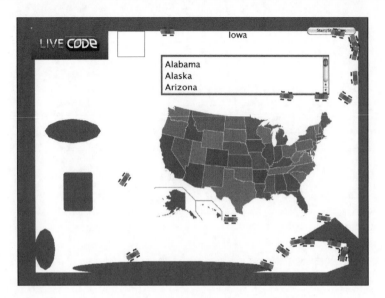

13. Note that you can continue to point at the parts of the image you first loaded (the LiveCode logo in the preceding example) to see the swatch to the right changing color. Also, if you point to different U.S. states, the text in the `state` field you created changes.

What just happened?

Having already used **imageData** to implement a color picker and to act as multiple button areas, we went on to use the **maskData** of the image as a collision map. There is quite a bit of arithmetic behind making the cars move in intelligent ways, and you could go on to change some of the numbers to get different behavior from the cars or you could take a break and get ready to make a jigsaw puzzle!

Pop quiz – calculate this!

For the U.S. map, we only needed to simulate 50 buttons. If you make use of the red, green, and blue values, how many buttons could you simulate?

1. One, enormous button
2. 65,536 buttons
3. 16,777,216 buttons

Answer: 3

As with the discussion about *bits and bytes* (hey, I'm sure we weren't going to see these words for the rest of this chapter!), the red, green, and blue values combine to give us 2 to the power of 24 possible values. If you only used two of the colors, then the answer would have been 65,536.

The things we have tried so far in this chapter use techniques that would be useful in any LiveCode application and are not specific to mobile applications. You can try the stack you have constructed; it will work well on a mobile device with 20 cars driving around the screen! The color picker and states map work on a mobile when its screen is touched. However, these tests don't really make use of the mobile features.

Making a jigsaw puzzle

The remainder of the chapter will build on the preceding information about `imageData` and will also take advantage of a few mobile device features. We will make a jigsaw puzzle app.

Going to pieces...

The general technique we're going to use, is to take a set of PNGs that have a nice alpha channel in them (that creates the puzzle piece edges) and then we will replace the actual pixel data with an image of our own. The first thing we need then is some PNGs.

If you want to make a commercial mobile application, either create your own puzzle shapes or buy a royalty free image. For prototyping, you could grab any image from the Web to get the basics going and then you could replace the images with higher quality ones that you have bought. Here, we are using a preview image from `http://depositphotos.com/`, which also sells higher quality versions.

When you do have high-quality versions, you may wish to create each puzzle piece, so that they touch against each other perfectly. Here, we're using a preview image, and we will select the inner part of each piece and create the PNGs from those. There will be small gaps between the pieces, but at least this way we can prepare the images we need quickly.

Time for action – creating the pieces and choosing an image

If you wish to follow along with the exact same image shown here, know that it was taken from the top-left section of the file present at:

```
http://static3.depositphotos.com/1004551/191/v/950/
depositphotos_1914748-Jigsaw-puzzle-blank-templates.jpg.
```

The image is shown here:

The following steps will help in creating the pieces and choosing an image:

1. Make a new Mainstack of the size 1024 x 768 (or the size of your tablet device). Name the stack `jigsaw`, set the title to `Jigsaw Puzzle`, and save it.

2. Open the whole puzzle image in your image editor.

3. Use the **Magic Wand** tool to pick up the inner part of the upper-left piece of the puzzle.

4. Fill that with a color that makes it easy to spot any remaining gaps.

5. Copy and paste into a new document (that has a transparent background) that is the size of the piece you copied.

6. Repair any gaps using the brush tool that is set to the same fill color.

7. Save it as a PNG file(with Photoshop, that would be save it for Web and devices, 24 bit, with transparency). Use a naming scheme that may help you identify the images easily. For example, `tlcorner.png`, `p1.png`, `trcorner.png`, and so on.

8. Proceed through all the differently shaped areas. In the example image, there will be as few as 14 unique shapes. No need to save other pieces that are of the same shape and orientation as the ones you already have.

9. The set of images will be similar to the ones shown in the following screenshot:

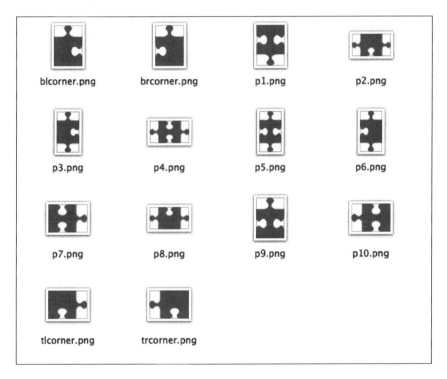

10. Import all the 14 images as **Control/Image**.

11. Lay out a puzzle that covers most of the card window. In the following screenshot, the puzzle was of 900 x 622 pixels with 11 x 8 pieces. Make duplicates of the middle piece images to fill in the whole puzzle. You can accurately place a piece after selecting it using the arrow keys on your keyboard.

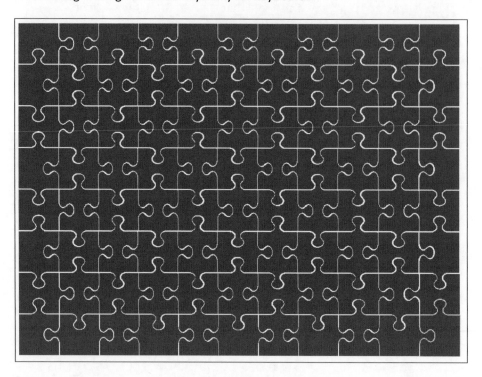

12. Name the images in a grid-like fashion. The top-left piece would be named `p 1 1`, the top-right edge piece would be named `p 11 1` and the bottom-right piece would have the name `p 11 8`.

13. Select all the pieces and group them. Name the group `pieces`.

14. Make a button with the name `fromcamera` and a label with the name `Take a Photo`. Set the button scripts to this:

```
on mouseUp
   loadimage "camera"
end mouseUp
```

Make another button, named "fromlibrary" and labeled "Load a Picture", with this script:

```
on mouseUp
   loadimage "library"
end mouseUp
```

15. Set the buttons to get a drop shadow; use the options in the **Graphic Effects** pane of the **Inspector** palette.

16. Edit the card script and add these global variables and functions that will initialize the values that will be needed by the other functions we'll make:

```
global originalimage, puzzlewidth, puzzleheight, snapdistance,
hcount, vcount


on opencard
   setvalues
end opencard


on setvalues
   put 900 into puzzlewidth
   put 662 into puzzleheight
   put 50 into snapdistance
   put 11 into hcount
   put 8 into vcount
end setvalues
```

17. Now, add the `loadImage` handler, which the two buttons will call in order to get an image from the user's camera or photo album:

```
on loadImage cameratype
  if puzzlewidth is empty then setvalues
  if there is an image "original" then delete image "original"
  mobilePickPhoto cameratype,puzzlewidth,puzzleheight
  if the result is empty then

    lock screen
    set the name of image the number of images to "original"
    set the width of image "original" to puzzlewidth
    set the height of image "original" to puzzleheight
    put the imageData of image "original" into originalImage
    delete image "original"
    --makepuzzle
    --scatter
    unlock screen
  else
    answer the result
  end if
end loadImage
```

18. The `makepuzzle` and `scatter` lines are commented out for now, so that you can test the functions so far.

What just happened?

The puzzle pieces are now in place and are named in a way that we can take advantage of them later when we manipulate them. If you go to **Standalone Application Settings** and select **iOS** or **Android**, you can give the app a try.

Setting up some test images

If you use the iPad Simulator, you won't be able to test getting an image from the camera, and at first, you will just have the default images in the photo library. To add your own photo, drag images from **Finder** to the Simulator window, and the image will be added to the Photos library. You can switch to the simulator Home screen to reselect the Jigsaw app using the *cmd + Shift + H* key combination. This way, you can add a few images to the library in order to select one as the picture for the puzzle.

When LiveCode gets an image from the mobile device, both from the camera and the library or photo album, it places the picture as an image control that is the topmost object on the card. We don't need the image itself, just its `imageData`. In the `loadImage` handler, the image is made in the same size as the puzzle pieces group, `imageData` is stored in the global variable `originalimage`, and the image itself is deleted.

Next, we'll transfer the chosen picture to the puzzle pieces.

Time for action – transferring imageData

By setting the chosen image to be of the same width and height as the group that holds the puzzle pieces (that's where the 900 and 662 numbers came from), it becomes possible for us to transfer the matching rectangle of data from the full image to the puzzle piece in question. The following steps will guide you in transferring imageData:

1. Open the card script again. Add the `makepuzzle` handler:

```
on makepuzzle
  resetpuzzle
  put the number of images in group "pieces" into imagecount
  repeat with a = 1 to imagecount
    makepiece the short name of image a of group "pieces"
  end repeat
end makepuzzle
```

2. The `makepuzzle` handler will go through each of the puzzle pieces and call another handler to do the transfer of data for that one piece. Here is the `makepiece` handler:

```
on makepiece piecename
  put the width of image piecename into piecewidth
  put the height of image piecename into pieceheight
  put empty into tempimage
  put the left of image piecename - the left of group "pieces"
into dx
  put the top of image piecename - the top of group "pieces" into
dy
  repeat with y = 1 to pieceheight
    put ((y+dy-1) * puzzlewidth + dx)*4 into sourcestart
    put char sourcestart+1 to sourcestart+piecewidth*4 of
originalimage after tempimage
  end repeat
  set the imageData of image piecename to tempimage
end makepiece
```

3. In the earlier `imageData` tests, we were only interested in one pixel at a time, but here, we want lots of rows of data. The arithmetic, *((y+dy-1) * puzzlewidth…*, and so on, quickly pull out a whole row of pixels at a time. These rows are built up into a new variable, `tempimage`, which is finally transferred into the actual puzzle piece.

4. After the pieces have their rectangle of `imageData`, we then need to move the pieces into random places, making the game ready for the user to play. This is done with a `scatter` handler:

```
on scatter
  repeat with a = 1 to the number of images in group "pieces"
    set the myloc of image a of group "pieces" to the loc of image
a of group "pieces"
    put the short name of image a of group "pieces" into n
    if edgepiece(n) then
      set the loc of image a of group "pieces" to 40 +
random(400),300 + random(400)
    else
      set the loc of image a of group "pieces" to 500 +
random(500),300 + random(400)
    end if
  end repeat
end scatter
```

5. The first thing that most jigsaw puzzle players do is they separate the *straight-edged* pieces. We can code things in a way so that their time is saved. We can employ a function that places the edge pieces away from the non-edge pieces. The `edgepiece` function (which is called from the preceding `scatter` handler) is this:

```
function edgepiece pName
   return word 2 of pName = 1 or word 3 of pName = 1 or word 2 of
pName = hcount or word 3 of pName = vcount
end edgepiece
```

6. The name that we carefully set for each piece is checked to verify that the piece is either at the left, right, top, or bottom edge of the puzzle. In other words, it's a piece located at the outer edges of the puzzle. Scatter places the straight-edged pieces in the left half of the screen and the others in the right half of the screen, as shown here:

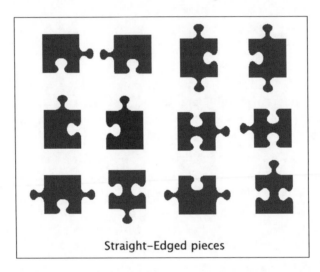

Straight-Edged pieces

7. The start of the `makepuzzle` handler calls a `resetpuzzle` handler that is used to make sure that the pieces are back where they started, ready for a new picture to load. This is achieved when you use a property variable on each piece named `myloc`, which records the initial location of the piece. Here's the `resetpuzzle` handler:

```
on resetpuzzle
   repeat with a = 1 to the number of images in group "pieces"
      if the myloc of image a of group "pieces" is not empty then
        set the loc of image a of group "pieces" to the myloc of
image a of group "pieces"
      else
        set the myloc of image a of group "pieces" to the loc of
image a of group "pieces"
```

```
      end if
   end repeat
end resetpuzzle
```

8. You can see that if `myloc` is not already set, then the piece must be in its start position, and so, the `resetpuzzle` handler goes ahead and records that location in the `myloc` property.

9. Uncomment the lines at step 17 of *Time for Action - creating the pieces and choosing an image* (`makepuzzle` and scatter lines) and try another test of the app. You should now be able to choose a picture and see it in the spread out puzzle pieces. Hopefully, you will see something like this:

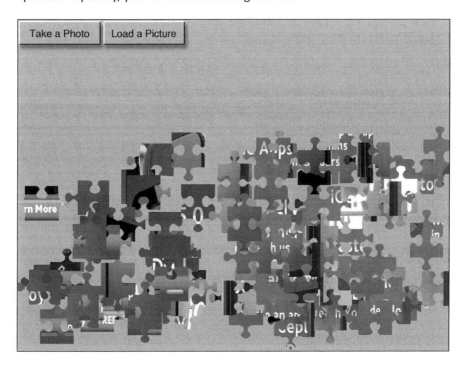

What just happened?

As mentioned in the preceding section, the right arithmetic made it relatively easy for us to extract a desired rectangle of `imageData` from a larger image, and store it in a smaller image that was the size of that rectangle. However, there's one bit of magic that wasn't pointed out, the puzzle kept its shape! Even though we had completely replaced `imageData` for the image, how did this happen? Setting `imageData` doesn't interfere with `alphaData` of the image. The PNGs that we imported kept their original alpha channel and so still had the same shape, but just a different image.

Adding interactivity

Our jigsaw puzzle is ready to be shipped! Well, other than the fact it has no interactivity at all! Let's add some.

Time for action – setting up touch events

The handlers so far have been in the card script, the plan being to have different cards with different types of puzzle. The interactivity handlers can be placed in the stack script available for all the cards.

1. Open the stack script. There is only one of the global variables that we will also need in the stack script, but there are a couple of initializing items we need to cover. Start the stack script with these lines:

```
global snapdistance

on preopenstack
  if the platform contains "iphone" then iphoneUseDeviceResolution
true
end preopenstack

on openstack
  set the compositorType of this stack to "Static OpenGL"
end openstack
```

2. The `preopenstack` handler checks whether the app is on iPhone and requests that the device's native resolution be used. This will make sure that Retina displays show the best quality. The `compositorType` being set to `"Static OpenGL"` will help performance.

3. The interactivity we'll use will make use of touch events. Each touch comes with an associated ID value. Here is the handler that detects the start of a touch event:

```
on touchStart touchid
  put the short name of the target into n
  if word 1 of n is "p" then
    set the dropShadow of image n to the dropShadow of button
"fromlibrary"
    set the relayerGroupedControls to true
    set the layer of the target to the number of images in group
"pieces"
  end if
end touchstart
```

4. The check of the target name is a quick way to make sure that we don't drag anything around except for the puzzle pieces. When a piece is touched, we use the `relayerGroupedControls` and layer functions to make that piece appear above the other pieces.

5. Do you remember how we added a dropshadow to the two buttons? Aside from making them look nicer, we make use of it here too. By adding the same `dropShadow` to the puzzle piece, we create the illusion that the piece is floating above the screen.

6. Next thing to watch for is movement, which we can do with the `touchMove` event:

```
on touchMove touchid,touchx,touchy
  put the short name of the target into n
  if word 1 of n is "p" then
    set the loc of the target to touchx,touchy
  end if
end touchMove
```

7. Again, there's a quick double check that you can perform to make sure that it's a puzzle piece; otherwise, it's a simple case of setting the location of the piece to the location of the user's finger.

8. When the user releases the piece, we check whether it's near its starting place, and if it is near, we move the piece into its place and remove the dropShadow effect:

```
on touchEnd touchid
  put the short name of the target into n
  if word 1 of n is "p" then
    checkdistance the short name of the target
    set the dropShadow of the target to empty
    checkfinished
  end if
end touchEnd
```

9. This is the `checkdistance` handler and a `distance` function that it calls:

```
on checkdistance dt
  if snapdistance is empty then put 100 into snapdistance
  put distance(item 1 of the loc of image dt - item 1 of the myloc
of image dt,item 2 of the loc of image dt - item 2 of the myloc of
image dt) into d
  if d<snapdistance then
    put max(.1,min(.2,d/200)) into t
    move image dt to the myloc of image dt in t seconds
    set the relayerGroupedControls to true
```

```
        set the layer of image dt to 2
    end if
end checkdistance

function distance dx,dy
   return sqrt(dx*dx+dy*dy)
end distance
```

10. The `distance` function is based on the **Pythagorean theorem**, returning the number of pixels between the puzzle piece and its original `myloc` value. `snapdistance` is the global variable that is used to determine whether the piece is close enough to its starting place to be considered on target.

11. The `move` line uses LiveCode's move function, which animates the piece into its place.

12. One last thing, let's check whether the puzzle is complete. Add this handler to the stack script:

```
on checkfinished
   repeat with a = 1 to the number of images in group "pieces"
     if the myloc of image a of group "pieces" <> the loc of image
a of group "pieces" then exit checkfinished
   end repeat
   answer "You've done it!"
end checkfinished
```

What just happened?

The jigsaw puzzle should fully work now. Something that you can't easily guess from the touch functions we added is the fact that it works with multitouch. You can drag on up to 10 pieces at once (or whatever the multitouch limit is for your device). Here, each piece will show a drop shadow and all the pieces will animate into their place when you let go of them.

Have a go hero – one for the kids

Functions that relate to the puzzle itself are in the card script. Try making a new card that has bigger puzzle pieces and a higher value for `snapdistance` (the higher the value, the easier it is to get a piece into place). You could make an opening card for the stack that has a set of difficulty level buttons, one of which would jump to the easier puzzle. This would be ideal for younger players.

Adding some guide graphics will help players know where the edges of the finished puzzle are, and for simpler difficulty levels, you can even include outlines of the individual puzzle pieces.

Summary

There are many other possibilities when it comes to making use of `imageData` in paint programs, image processing applications, and so on, and it is still the same as in the preceding examples. In this chapter, we went over and understood the format of `imageData`, `alphaData`, and `maskData` and how to copy areas of `imageData` from one image to another. Reading individual pixels of an image and finding novel uses for the pixel values was covered here as well. We also saw how to use multitouch interactivity to bring those chunks of `imageData` to life in the form of a jigsaw puzzle.

Working with graphics can be great fun, hopefully, this will just be the start of what you will create. However, in the next chapter, we'll get back to making a utility application. Sigh...

6
Making a Reminder Application

Note to self...

To-do lists, alarms, birthday reminders, notes, shopping lists, and the list goes on. There should be an app to keep a list of the different apps that keep lists! At the time of writing this book, there were already over 8,000 iOS apps that were lists, planners, or alarms. Perhaps, there's room for one more...

It could take a lot of research, and money, to explore all the reminder apps that are out there. The majority of apps will have a lot of features that you'll never use and at least one vital feature that is missing. If you're lucky, some combination of apps may do all the things you want in a reminder. However, don't forget that you use LiveCode and can make your own reminder app!

In this chapter, we will:

◆ Discuss what is meant by a *reminder*

◆ Create some time measuring utility functions

◆ Define a data structure to store information about an event

◆ Make use of mobile device "notifications"

◆ Create a flexible reminder app

Different types of reminders

Here is the list of a few of the things that you might call a "reminder":

- A shopping list
- A Christmas present list
- A to-do list
- An alarm clock
- An egg timer
- A birthday reminder

Now, is there a single way to describe all of these things? Well, it may get wordy, but a reminder could be described as a notification message or sound that either appears automatically or shows when you look for it. It is used to let you know that a certain time has passed, a moment has arrived, or that an outstanding task has not been completed.

See, pretty wordy. Breaking it down like this helps us to see what features a reminder app will need to have. Before getting to that, let's test the definition against the preceding examples:

A shopping list: In this case, you go looking for the reminder. Although, we could set it up to automatically show when your location happens to be near the store! Other than that, this is effectively a task that has not been completed.

A Christmas present list: This is much the same as a shopping list, but it could use a timed message that let's you know how few shopping days are left for you to buy a Christmas present for your loved ones.

A to-do list: Again, this is simply a list of tasks that are not yet complete.

An alarm clock: This gives you a notification that a moment in time has been reached.

An egg timer: This is a notification of a certain amount of time that has passed, which could be used as a sequence of such events that might be used in a cooking-buddy app.

A birthday reminder: This shows whether a certain moment has been reached. Really though, you want to set the reminder so that it can notify you ahead of the actual event.

At least as a starting point, we can use the definition to guide us as we outline the abilities the app will need to have.

Timing of notifications

The mobile notifications that can be created with LiveCode will be sent the moment you ask for it to be sent. Strangely though, the value is based on the number of seconds since midnight on January 1st, 1970, specifically, in part of London! Well, it's named after an area of London called Greenwich.

Greenwich Mean Time, often referred to as **GMT**, has been used as the standard for measuring time. It is somewhat superseded by **UTC (Coordinated Universal Time)**, but in either case, it represents the exact current time at least for countries that are within the same time zone as Greenwich. The rest of us add or subtract some amount of time from that value.

In order to adapt to the fact that the Earth doesn't go around the Sun in an exact number of days or even an exact number of quarter days, calendars are adjusted by one day every four years, though not on 100 year boundaries, except for every 400 years (for example, the year 2000 was a leap year). These adjustments are still not enough to keep the clocks on time! The clocks are out of time by about 0.6 seconds a year, and so there are "Leap Seconds" added to compensate for that. In theory, Leap Seconds could be used to subtract one second, but as of yet, this hasn't been needed, as they have only been used to add one second.

None of this affects the number of seconds since midnight of January 1, 1970, but it does mean that converting LiveCode's **seconds** into time and date using your own arithmetic won't give you the right time. Yet, it's still used as the basis for notifications. This value is usually referred to as Unix Time.

It doesn't matter much though if you end up sending someone a Happy Birthday message 25 seconds early! Don't worry, the way we'll calculate the notification time will take care of the oddity.

Date and time pickers

As mentioned in the preceding section, mobile notifications use the number of seconds since midnight of January 1, 1970 and don't add on the 25 seconds, or Leap Seconds, that have occurred since then. When we present the date and time pickers to the user, the selections the user makes will come back as the actual current or future time. We will adjust for that later.

Time for action – creating date and time pickers

Let's make another test-rig stack, which we'll use to try out some date and time pickers:

1. Create a new Mainstack, name it `ReminderFunctions`, and save the stack.

2. Add two fields and two new buttons.

3. Name one field `dateinseconds` and the other `timeinseconds`.

4. Name the buttons as `Pick Date` and `Pick Time`.

5. Set the script of the **Pick Date** button to this:

```
on mouseUp
  mobilePickDate date
  put the result into tDate
  convert tDate to seconds
  put tDate into field "dateinseconds"
end mouseUp
```

6. Set the **Pick Time** button script to this:

```
on mouseUp
  mobilePickDate "time"
  put the result into tTime
  convert tTime to seconds
  put tTime into field timeinseconds
end mouseUp
```

7. Set the Standalone Application Settings so that you can test on iOS or Android.

8. Choose your **Test Target** (in the following steps, you can see that the iPhone simulator was chosen in this case) and do a **Test**.

9. Click on the **Pick Date** button.

10. Select `December 25th, 2012` and click on **Done**.

11. The number of seconds from midnight of January 1, 1970 to midnight of Christmas day 2012 will be shown in the first field that you created.

12. Click on the **Pick Time** button and set the time to `1` am. The following image shows how the picker looks different on iOS and the Android simulator:

13. Click on **Done** and you will see the number of seconds from midnight of January 1 1970 to 1 AM of the day you do this test in the right-hand side field.

What just happened?

We just made two simple scripts that call the native date or time picker and convert the result into seconds to then show them in a field. What is interesting to note is that for the Pick Time case, it doesn't return the number of seconds of the current day, that is, all the seconds since midnight of January 1, 1970. In order to set a notification time for a particular time of a particular date, we have to do a little arithmetic. We'll go into that a little later when we make the actual reminder app in the *Making the reminders app* section of this chapter.

Pop quiz – OA (odd acronyms!)

You may have noticed that the acronym for "Coordinated Universal Time" is UTC and not CUT. Why is that?

1. CUT is too common a word.

2. So as not to upset the French.

3. The acronym committee members were dyslexics.

Answer: 2

The French may not have proactively objected, but indeed, the acronym of UTC was chosen so as to not specifically match the English version of the phrase. It also fell in nicely with the other acronyms such as UT0, UT1, and so on.

Where?

There is something we can do in a mobile reminder app that would never work in a pen and paper version of a reminder; we can present the list of reminders based on where you are at the time that you check it! To make use of location, you need to know where you are now and how far your location is from the place associated with the reminder.

At the time of writing this book, there was no ability in LiveCode to directly pull in a map so that you could choose locations other than the one you are at right now. So, we'll work within that limitation.

 That being said, there is `mergMK` external (for more information, refer to `http://mergext.com`), which works with iOS versions before 7.0 and was being updated at the time of writing this book. You could also use a combination of HTML and JavaScript as described in the article at `http://stackoverflow.com/questions/25629786/fetch-data-from-html-file-in-livecode`. However, these are both beyond the scope of this beginner's book

The general technique while reading a mobile device's sensors, is to start tracking a given sensor, detect when changes happen, and to stop tracking the sensor. You can take a reading from the sensor at any time between the start and stop tracking commands. You can also specify how detailed a report you want and whether you want a precise reading. The precise reading of the location would dictate whether GPS was used or not. The advantage of using GPS is that you get greater accuracy (assuming there's a clear signal at the time) and the disadvantages are that it uses more battery power, and devices that don't have GPS cannot use this feature. When using location as part of a reminder, we're mainly interested in whether you're at home, the office, or perhaps at the supermarket. So, we'll use the less precise reading, the GPS one would be an overkill.

Time for action – trying out native location tracking

Later in this chapter, we will add in a feature to allow the app user to add a set of favorite locations. For the moment, we'll just try out the basic functions. Location doesn't work in the simulators; you'll have to try this on a real device:

1. Use the test-rig stack from the preceding steps and add a `Get Location` button and a `location` field. Make sure that the `location` field is as wide as the card window; it will show three long numbers.

2. Set the script of the button to the following:

```
on mouseUp
  mobileStartTrackingSensor "location", true
  put mobileSensorReading("location", false) into field "location"
  mobileStopTrackingSensor "location"
end mouseUp
```

3. The `true` value in the second line is the one that defines a *loosely* value saying that we don't need the precision of GPS. The `false` value in the third line says that we don't need detailed information to be returned.

4. Go to **Standalone Application Settings** and choose your target device as **iOS** or **Android**.

5. For iOS, set the **Display Name**, **Internal App ID**, and **Profile**. Choose your device and SDK version):

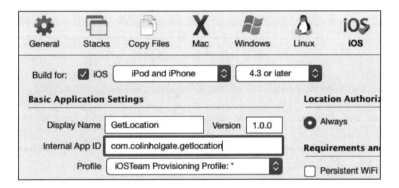

6. Also, in the iOS **Requirements and Restrictions** section, select **Location Services** and **GPS** as required. In the app, you will also have to accept Location Services when iOS prompts for it.

7. For Android, set the **Label**, **Identifier**, and **Minimum Android Version** fields:

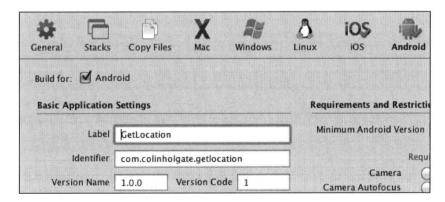

8. Additionally, in the **Application Permissions** part of the Android settings, make sure that you have asked permission to get the **Coarse Location** permission:

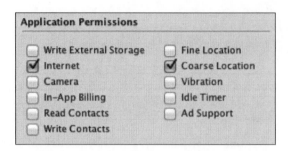

9. Select **Save Standalone Application** and install the app onto your device. Follow the description given in *Chapter 2, Getting Started with LiveCode Mobile* if you need a reminder on how to do that!

10. In the app, try the **Pick Date** and **Pick Time** buttons to see how they bring up the native controls and then click on the **Get Location** button. Three long numbers should appear in the location field:

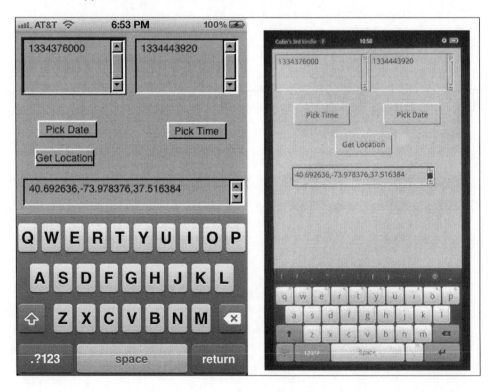

What just happened?

As you can see, there is very little code needed to read a location! If this was a tracking app, you would need to keep the tracking open and have functions to respond to the change of location messages, but for our app, we just need to know where you are at the time you take a look at your list of reminders.

The numbers that are shown in the location field are the latitude, longitude, and elevation of the position of the device. However, how will we use these numbers...?

Calculating the distance between two points on the Earth

The plan is to make your app able to sort your reminders list in order of distance from where you are right now. Let's say you really use this app a lot and have dozens of reminders. The reminder you created about buying some bread may be at the bottom of the list, but if you have assigned the location of the supermarket to that reminder, sorting the list while you're outside the supermarket should bring the shopping list items to the top.

When faced with a problem such as this one, how will you come to know the distance between two points on Earth; Google is a good starting place for you to find that out! It takes very little research and time to find:

`http://www.movable-type.co.uk/scripts/latlong.html`

The article in this URL discusses the original formula for calculating this and then shows a JavaScript function. If you find it hard to convert the equation into LiveCode handlers, you ought to be able to convert the JavaScript, line by line, into the LiveCode equivalent.

No need to type this in just yet, we'll integrate it later; however, if you want to have a play, put these lines into the stack script:

```
function distance lat1,lon1,lat2,lon2
  put 6371 into r
  put toRad((lat2-lat1)) into dLat
  put toRad((lon2-lon1)) into dLon
  put toRad(lat1) into lat1
  put toRad(lat2) into lat2
  put sin(dLat/2) * sin(dLat/2) + sin(dLon/2)*sin(dLon/2) *
cos(lat1)*cos(lat2) into a
  put 2*atan2(sqrt(a),sqrt(1-a)) into c
  put r*c into d
  return d
end distance

function toRad pAngle
  return pAngle/180*PI
end toRad
```

Try this in the message box:

```
put distance(40,-74,51,0)
```

This appears as shown in the following screenshot:

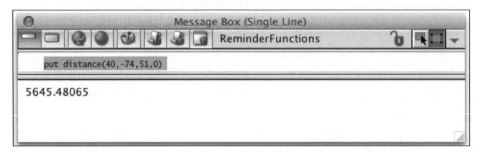

As shown in the preceding screenshot, you should see a value of **5645.48065**. The two locations are somewhere near New York and London, and that value would be the distance in kilometers between the two along the surface of the Earth.

Pop quiz – what floor is my apartment on?

Examine the screenshot (the one timed "6:53 PM", which precedes the previous screenshot), and given the clue that the building I live in is not much above sea level, which floor do I live on?

1. 40th floor
2. 73 floors below ground
3. 11th floor
4. I'm homeless

Answer: 3

The numbers coming back from the location sensor return as latitude, longitude, and elevation. This would make the elevation on where the device was at that time be about 37.5 meters, which is much too low to be the 40th floor. There is enough information in the screenshot for you to know exactly when it was taken and where on Earth!

Information needed in a reminder

We're well on the way to know how to set a time and date for the reminder notification to occur, and we will be able to sort the reminders based on the distance from where we are. However, what exact information do we need in the reminder itself?

If this were a birthday reminder app, you would just need to ask for the person's name and the date of their birthday. If it were a shopping list app, you would need the name of the item and maybe the quantity. For a timer, you would need to ask what the event is called and would need to set a time for the event.

Here though, we're trying to make a completely flexible reminder app; it would be up to the user to describe the item in whatever manner they wish. So, we'll just ask for a title and a brief description. We will also need to offer the option of setting a date, time, an associated location, and whether an alert sound should be played.

Another thing to think about is; where will we store the information for the list of reminders? While making the WebScraper app in *Chapter 4, Using Remote Data and Media*, we chose to duplicate the main application stack into the documents folder and to then jump into that copy of the stack. This enabled the ability to save changes to the stack. The reminder app is a simpler case; we're only trying to store a few text strings to define each reminder and it would be simpler to just write a text file using this app.

We want to allow the user to make a list of locations, so that a reminder can be associated with that location. Rather than writing a different text file, we will make the first piece of information in each entry be the function of that entry. Right now, the only two functions are `location` and `reminder`. The following is an example of how the text file might look:

```
Location   Home   40.692636   -73.978376
Location   Office   40.745194   -73.985199
Reminder   Packt   Ask for more time!   1334548800   Home   false
Reminder   Boss   Buy lunch      1334592000   Office   true
```

Between each item in the line is a tab character, which will be used to separate the parts of the entry. The structure for a location is:

- Function: `Location`
- Location's title
- Latitude
- Longitude

For a reminder, it's:

1. Function: `Reminder`
2. Title
3. Brief description
4. Notification time in seconds since midnight of January 1, 1970
5. A location associated with this reminder
6. Whether to play an alert sound (`true` or `false`)

Making the reminder app

Ok, enough groundwork! Let's start making the reminder app. Rather than adding a feature at the time, along with any scripts, we'll make the various cards that will be needed to create the app's **GUI (graphical user interface)** first and then go back and add the scripts.

Laying out the cards

We're going to make the first card of the stack be a place where you can see the current reminders, sort them by time or location, and add new reminders and locations. Then, we will make a second card to enter the location details and a third card to enter the details for a new reminder.

Time for action – creating the reminder app screens

The steps shown here are going to use the standard LiveCode fields and buttons, but feel free to make your version more attractive!

1. Create a new Mainstack, give it the name `EasyReminder`, and save it. Other names, such as `Simple Reminders`, might be more descriptive, but it would be too long a name if you're using an older iPhone.

2. Set the card size to the size of your device. The screenshots shown in this section are based on an older iPhone-sized stack.

3. Go to **Standalone Application Settings** and set the values in the same way that we did while testing the **Location** feature.

4. Set the name of the first card to be `home`.

5. Create a **Sort by Time** button, a **Sort by Location** button, one field named `reminders`, another field named `data`, and two buttons named `Create Reminder...` and `Create Location...`.

6. Add one more button named `Delete Location or Reminder`.

7. Make sure that both the fields have their **Lock text** and **Don't wrap** box checked.

8. You should now have a screen that looks something like the following screenshot:

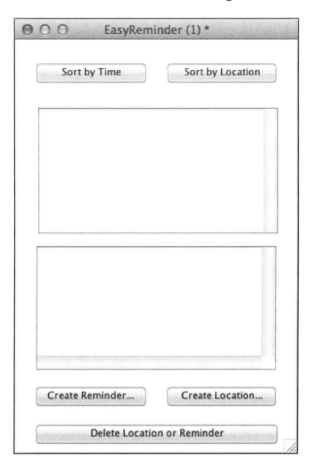

9. Make a new card and name it `location`.

10. Add a field and set its contents to: `Enter the latitude and longitude for this location`.

11. Add two input fields named `latitude`, and `longitude`.

12. Create a button named `Set to Current Location`.

Avoid typos

Although we have placed a field for you to type in the location by hand, use the **Set to Current Location** button if possible or at least use that at your current location to see the format that is required.

13. Add another instructions field that says: `Enter a name for this location:`.

14. Add a third input field named `location name`. Note that on older phones with smaller screens, this field location needs to be toward the top of the screen, so that it isn't covered by the keyboard popup.

15. Finally, add a button named `Add Location` and `Cancel`.

16. For this card, all the three fields need their **Lock text** box to be unchecked.

17. The card should look like the following screenshot:

18. Make a third card and name it `reminder`.

19. Add two instructions fields that say: `Enter a title for this reminder:` and `Enter a brief description:`.

20. Create two more input fields named `title`, and `description`.

21. Create three buttons named `Set Related Location`, `Set Date`, and `Set Time`.

22. Add three fields next to those buttons, which will be used to show the user that the selection they made has taken place. Name the fields `location field`, `date field`, and `time field`.

23. Create a checkbox button named `Play Alert Sound`.

24. Lastly, create two more buttons named `Add Reminder` and `Cancel`.

25. Arrange all of these elements to appear as shown in the following screenshot:

What just happened?

We've made all of the screens needed for the app to function. That was the easy bit. Just wait until you see how much typing you are going to do!

Stack-level scripts

There is quite a bit of code ahead. Describing it feature by feature would require us to jump all over the place , which would add to the existing scripts in some cases and we would easily get lost in this situation. So, instead of doing it that way, we'll look at the code for each card at a time and also at the handlers that go into the stack script. It's shown here in the *Time for action* section, mainly to give you a break now and then! Without further ado, the stack script...

Time for action – adding stack-level functions

For this app, we're going to put some of the logic in the buttons on the cards themselves, but it still leaves a good amount that will have to go into the Stack script. To make it less overwhelming, we'll show one or two functions at a time followed by some explanation about any interesting points in the following steps:

1. Open the Stack script.

2. Type in the the following handlers:

```
on openstack
   if the platform is "iphone" then iPhoneSetKeyboardReturnKey
"done"
   readdata
   showdata
end openstack

on returnInField
   focus on nothing
end returnInField
```

Android OS keyboards generally have a button dedicated to the function putting the keyboard away. On iOS, this isn't the case, as the button that sits where the *Return* key should be, may have a special word instead, such as *Send*, or *Done*. Unfortunately, we are entering text into fields that are able to take a return character. To solve the issue, we set the Return button to say *Done*, which will lead the user to expect the keyboard to go away when that button is pressed. We will also trap the `returnInField` message and use it as a way to actually put the keyboard away.

3. Next, type in the functions that will read, and write the list of reminders as a text file to the documents folder on your device:

```
on writedata
   global gReminderData
   put specialFolderPath("documents") & "/reminders.txt" into
tRemindersPath
   if gReminderData is empty then put "no entries yet" into
gReminderData
   open file tRemindersPath
   write gReminderData to file tRemindersPath
```

```
    close file tRemindersPath
    clearnotifiers
    setupnotifiers
end writedata


on readdata
  global gReminderData
  put specialFolderPath("documents") & "/reminders.txt" into
tRemindersPath
  if there is a file tRemindersPath then
      open file tRemindersPath
      read from file tRemindersPath until eof
      close file tRemindersPath
      put it into gReminderData
  else
      open file tRemindersPath
      write "no entries yet" to file tRemindersPath
      close file tRemindersPath
      put "no entries yet" into gReminderData
  end if
end readdata
```

> These two functions are using the straightforward ability
> that LiveCode has to read and write text files. Note that
> `specialFolderPath` is being used to help work out where
> the file will be saved. This works even when you test on desktop
> machines. The LiveCode Dictionary shows a full list of special
> folder paths, including many that don't apply to mobile apps.

4. You can put the following `showdata` function into the Home card's Card script as well, but having it in the Stack level keeps it near other functions that are related to it. Type it in now:

```
on showdata
  global gReminderData
  go card "home"
  put empty into field "reminders"
  put gReminderData into field "data"
  if gReminderData = "no entries yet" then
    exit showdata
  end if
  set the itemdelimiter to tab
```

```
    put 1 into tLineNumber
    repeat with a = 1 to the number of lines in gReminderData
       put line a of gReminderData into tEntry
       if item 1 of tEntry = "Reminder" then
          put item 2 of tEntry into tTitle
          put item 3 of tEntry into tDescription
          put item 4 of tEntry into tNotificationTime
          convert tNotificationTime from seconds to abbreviated time
and long date
          put item 5 of tEntry into tLocationName
          put tTitle & ":" && tDescription && tNotificationTime &&
tLocationName into line tLineNumber of field "reminders"
          add 1 to tLineNumber
       end if
    end repeat
end showdata
```

> If you recall the sample text file from earlier, the showdata
> function takes each line and splits the tab delimited items into
> chunks of information to present to the user. One cute trick is
> that the notification time, which is a long number of seconds,
> is converted into a human-readable form, showing both the
> date and time of the notification. The data field is used to
> show the raw data that has been saved. In the final application,
> you would not show this, but it's handy to check whether the
> reminder information looks correct or not.

5. The last functions in the Stack script are used to set up the notifications themselves:

```
on clearnotifiers
   mobileCancelAllLocalNotifications
end clearnotifiers

on setupnotifiers
   global gReminderData
   if gReminderData = "no entries yet" then exit setupnotifiers
   set the itemdelimiter to tab
   repeat with a = 1 to the number of lines in gReminderData
      put line a of gReminderData into tEntryDetails
      if item 1 of tEntryDetails = "Reminder" then
         put item 2 of tEntryDetails && "-" && item 3 of
tEntryDetails into alertBody
```

```
      put "OK" into alertButtonMessage
      put tEntryDetails into alertPayload
      put item 4 of tEntryDetails into alertTime
      put item 6 of tEntryDetails into playSound
      mobileCreateLocalNotification alertBody, alertButtonMessage,
alertPayload, alertTime, playSound
    end if
  end repeat
end setupnotifiers

on localNotificationReceived pMsg
  answer "Local Notification:" && pMsg
end localNotificationReceived
```

Many mobile apps that use notifications don't ever clear them. In general, maybe they don't need to be cleared. Once they go by, they're gone for good! Well, not always. Sometimes, you'll go into an app just ahead of when a notification comes and you'd do the task, only to then be pestered with notifications about something you already did! In our app, we clear all the notifications that were due and recreate the whole list again. This way, any that you have deleted won't come back to haunt you later. To help in debugging, `alertPayload` is filled in with the entire reminder entry and will be shown to you when the notification comes in.

What just happened?

In addition to getting your fingers nicely warmed up, you entered all the functions to read and write the reminders data and to create and receive the notification messages.

Home card scripts

We're not going to put any scripts into the card level; they can just be inside various buttons. Starting with the ones on the first card.

Time for action – making the home card buttons work

The **Sort by Location** button's script is quite something. You should look forward to that! First, we'll start with the **Sort by Time** button:

1. Edit the script of the **Sort by Time** button on the first card.

2. Type in the following short handler:

```
on mouseUp
   global gReminderData
   set the itemdelimiter to tab
   sort gReminderData numeric by item 4 of each
   showdata
   writedata
end mouseUp
```

 LiveCode's sort command is powerful and in the preceding case, it sorts the list of reminders based on the notification seconds value. Once the lines are sorted, the list is recreated for the user to see and the text file is rewritten.

3. Get mentally prepared and then edit the script of the **Sort by Location** button.

4. Type in all of the following lines of code:

```
on mouseUp
   global gReminderData
   mobileStartTrackingSensor "location", true
   put mobileSensorReading("location", false) into tLocation
   mobileStopTrackingSensor "location"
   set the itemdelimiter to comma
   put item 1 of tLocation into tLat
   put item 2 of tLocation into tLong
   set the itemdelimiter to tab
   sort gReminderData numeric by getdistance(tLat,tLong,item 5 of
each)
   showdata
   writedata
end mouseUp


function getdistance pLat,pLong,pLocName
   if pLocName is empty then return 1000000
   global gReminderData
   put empty into tLat
   put empty into tLong
   repeat with a = 1 to the number of lines in gReminderData
      if item 1 of tEntryDetails = "Location" then
         if item 2 of tEntryDetails = pLocName then
            put item 3 of tEntryDetails into tLat
            put item 4 of tEntryDetails into tLong
         end if
```

```
      end if
    end repeat
    if tLat is empty then return 1000000000
    return distance(tLat,tLong,pLat,pLong)
  end getdistance

  function distance lat1,lon1,lat2,lon2
    put 6371 into r
    put toRad((lat2-lat1)) into dLat
    put toRad((lon2-lon1)) into dLon
    put toRad(lat1) into lat1
    put toRad(lat2) into lat2
    put sin(dLat/2) * sin(dLat/2) + sin(dLon/2)*sin(dLon/2) *
  cos(lat1)*cos(lat2) into a
    put 2*atan2(sqrt(a),sqrt(1-a)) into c
    put r*c into d
    return d
  end distance

  function toRad pAngle
    return pAngle/180*PI
  end toRad
```

The first part of the mouseUp handler just gets your current location. The distance and toRad functions are the same ones we looked at earlier. The magic happens in the way that the sort line uses a function to determine the sort order. By passing the Location that you associated with each reminder into the getdistance function, it's possible to run through the list of locations to find a match and to then use that location's latitude and longitude to measure the distance from your current location. This distance is then used by the sort command to decide the order of the lines.

5. For a moment's relaxation, edit the **Create Reminder...** button script and set it to this:

```
on mouseUp
  go to card "reminder"
end mouseUp
```

6. Likewise, set the **Create Location...** button script to the following:

```
on mouseUp
  go to card "location"
end mouseUp
```

7. For the last script for this card, edit the **Delete Location or Reminder** button script and type the following in:

```
on mouseUp
  global gReminderData
  mobilePick gReminderData,1,"checkmark","cancelDone","picker"
  put the result into tItemsToDelete
  if tItemsToDelete = "0" then exit mouseUp
  set the itemdelimiter to comma
  repeat with a = the number of items in tItemsToDelete down to 1
    delete line (item a of tItemsToDelete) of gReminderData
  end repeat
  if gReminderData is empty then put "no entries yet" into
gReminderData
  showdata
  writedata
end mouseUp
```

> The delete handler uses `mobilePick` with a particular set of parameters. One interesting parameter is `checkmark`. Asking for that type of picker will then show a list with checkboxes in it when you're on iPad or Android. That would enable you to choose several entries to delete in one go. Hence, the repeat loop that goes through as many items as you choose.

What just happened?

All being well, you have recovered by now after trying to understand the sort-by-location function! You can at least see how tough the Stack script would have been if all of this code would have been placed in that one location. Let's go on to the next card...

Creating a location card

Next up, we will create the card that we will show when the user touches the **Create a Location...** button on the first card.

Time for action – making the location card work

The Location card has three fields in it for latitude, longitude, and a title for the location. The user could type in the details manually, but if they happen to be at the location in question, there's a button there that will grab the location and fill in the numbers automatically. The following steps will guide you in making the location card work:

1. Edit the script of the **Set to Current Location** button and type in the following lines of code:

```
on mouseUp
  mobileStartTrackingSensor "location", true
  put mobileSensorReading("location", false) into tLocation
  mobileStopTrackingSensor "location"
  set the itemdelimiter to comma
  if the number of items in tLocation = 3 then
    put item 1 of tLocation into field "latitude"
    put item 2 of tLocation into field "longitude"
  end if
end mouseUp
```

2. Nothing too tricky here; we just captured the location and stored the latitude and longitude entries in the two fields.

3. Edit the script of the **Cancel** button and change it to the following easy script:

```
on mouseUp
  go to card "home"
end mouseUp
```

4. For the last item for this card, edit the **Add Location** button script and type in the following code:

```
on mouseUp
  global gReminderData
  if field "location name" is empty then
    answer "Please enter a name for this location."
    exit mouseUp
  end if
  if field "latitude" is empty or field "longitude" is empty then
    answer "Please enter location values, or press the 'Set to
Current Location' button."
    exit mouseUp
  end if
```

```
        put "Location" & tab & field "location name" & tab & field
    "latitude" & tab & field "longitude" into tLocationDetails
        if gReminderData = "no entries yet" then
          put tLocationDetails into gReminderData
        else
          put return & tLocationDetails after gReminderData
        end if
        go to card "home"
        showdata
        writedata
    end mouseUp
```

Most of the handler just checks whether the user entered the required information.

What just happened?

A lot less has happened than what happened on the first card! However, it was important all the same. Now, we have a way where the user can set up a location to be used by the reminders that they have created. That's where we're headed now...

The reminder entry form

This last card is essentially an entry form; we just want to ask the user what the reminder is for. There are some tricky aspects to it though and one or two lengthy functions to cope with that.

Time for action – taking in information about the reminder

The Reminder card makes good use of pickers. There is little typing for the user to do, and because they pick an entry from a list we present, there's a good chance the information won't have any typos in it! Use the following steps for taking in information about the reminder:

1. Edit the script of the **Set Related Location** button and type in the following lines of code:

```
on mouseUp
   global gReminderData
   put empty into tLocations
   set the itemdelimiter to tab
   put 1 into tLineNumber
   repeat with a = 1 to the number of lines in gReminderData
      if item 1 of line a of gReminderData = "Location" then
         put item 2 to 4 of line a of gReminderData into line
tLineNumber of tLocations
```

```
        add 1 to tLineNumber
      end if
    end repeat
    if tLocations is empty then
      answer "You need to add a location."
    else
      mobilePick tLocations,1
      put the result into tChosenLocation
      if tChosenLocation >0 then
        put item 1 of line tChosenLocation of tLocations into field
"location field"
      end if
    end if
end mouseUp
```

 We made the first word of each line in the reminders data either Location or Reminder. Here's one place where we can make use of that. Once we pull out the lines that are "Location", presenting them inside a picker is easy.

2. Edit the script of the **Set Date** button and change it to the following easy-to-understand script:

```
on mouseUp
  mobilePickDate "date"
  put the result into tDate
  convert tDate to seconds
  put tDate into field "date field"
end mouseUp
```

3. Set the script of the **Set Time** button to the following, which is almost an identical script:

```
on mouseUp
  mobilePickDate "time"
  put the result into tTime
  convert tTime to seconds
  put tTime into field "time field"
end mouseUp
```

4. The **Cancel** button script is the same as it is on the Location card given here:

```
on mouseUp
  go to card "home"
end mouseUp
```

5. Last, and far from least, the **Add Reminder** button script does all the hard work:

```
on mouseUp
  global gReminderData
  if field "title" is empty or field "description" is empty then
    answer "Please enter both a title and a description."
    exit mouseUp
  end if
  put "false" into tDoAlert
  if the hilite of button "Play Alert Sound" then put "true" into
tDoAlert
  put field "date field" into tDateValue
  put field "time field" into tTimeValue
  convert tTimeValue from seconds to short date
  convert tTimeValue to seconds
  put field "time field" - tTimeValue into tTimeValue
  add tTimeValue to tDateValue
  put "Reminder" & tab & field "title" & tab & field "description"
into tReminderDetails
  put tReminderDetails & tab & tDateValue & tab & field "location
field" & tab into tReminderDetails
  put tReminderDetails & tab & tDoAlert into tReminderDetails
  if gReminderData = "no entries yet" then
    put tReminderDetails into gReminderData
  else
    put return & tReminderDetails after gReminderData
  end if
  go to card "home"
  showdata
  writedata
end mouseUp
```

Most of the preceding script just combines the different bits of information together into one reminder entry with the parts delimited with a tab character. However, there is one bit of cute arithmetic going on in there too. At the start of this chapter, we looked at how Unix Time differs from the actual time at a rate of 0.6 seconds per year. If you want to set a notification at 8 AM five years from now, you can't take the value that the Set Time button gave you because that refers to today's 8 AM. You can't take the value that Set Date gave you because that would be midnight. So, by converting the time value to the short date format and then back to the seconds format, you can find out what the Unix Time was at midnight of the current day. Subtracting that from the value that Set Time gave you let's you know the number of seconds since midnight, regardless of how many seconds behind Unix Time is. Adding that value to the one from Set Date will give us an exact Unix Time in seconds for the notification to occur. Under iOS, there is a picker type that allows you to set the date and time together, but as that isn't on Android, we've used a way that works for both.

What just happened?

Phew! We got to the end! Try to run the app on your device. If your fingers aren't too numb, that is! Honestly, you could bet a fortune that it won't work the first time, but if it works well enough to show the raw text in the data field on the first card, hopefully, you'll be able to track down any errors in the code. You can also type in some test data into the stack on your computer and at least test the functions that don't require device-specific features.

Have a go hero – nice transitions

Really, if you've managed to get through and entered all that code to the point that the app is working, you're already a hero! However, read the section in the iOS and Android release notes for LiveCode about *Visual effects support*. Check whether you can get some typical mobile OS transitions happening as you go to and from the different cards.

Summary

This chapter was way more exciting than expected! A reminder app is absolutely not quite as impressive as Angry Birds, but making use of the location features of a mobile device makes it a little more novel. Along the way, we covered the process of reading and writing data to the special documents folder as well as the use of pickers for straightforward lists, dates, and time. We also showed how to read the current location of the device and how to set up local notification events.

In the best of cases, you can manage to make a mobile app in a few hours or a few days, but there is quite a lot that goes on before you can submit the app to the various app stores. Sounds like a good topic for the next chapter!

7
Deploying to Your Device

Don't keep it all to yourself!

Tools such as LiveCode can be used entirely for personal productivity applications, and it would more than pay for itself through the time that it would save every day. However, why not let the rest of the world benefit from your creations!

So far, we have created several little test rig apps and a few apps that are fleshed out. In all cases though, we've just tested the apps that are inside simulators or on your personal device. The time has come to get this app out to more people for beta testing at first, so that we can then upload it to different app stores.

In this chapter, we will:

◆ Examine all the standalone application setting options related to the process of creating mobile apps

◆ Create builds of an app so that it can be sent to beta testers

◆ Test service alternatives

◆ Build the final distribution version of an app

◆ Review how to upload apps to iOS App Store, Google Play, Amazon Appstore, and Samsung Apps

There are some stages that should be performed on Mac while creating iOS apps for App Store; all the iOS steps described here should be followed using Mac. The Android steps can be applied to Mac or Windows. Note that this chapter is more of a reference and not a hands-on walkthrough. When you have an app that is almost complete and ready for submission to app stores and if you get stuck at any point, hopefully, you will recall reading about the issue somewhere in this chapter!

Standalone application settings

We have already tweaked the settings a few times by now, but we've only made the minimum amount of changes needed to test the app. There are a lot of options here that you need to fill before your app is ready for sale in an app store. We'll briefly go over the other standalone application sections and then go into more depth in the Android and iOS sections.

The General section

The **General** section of the standalone settings is primarily used to control the features of LiveCode that are to be included in a desktop standalone application. These options cannot be applied to mobile applications, but it is in the **General** section that you can set the name of the application file and the build folder:

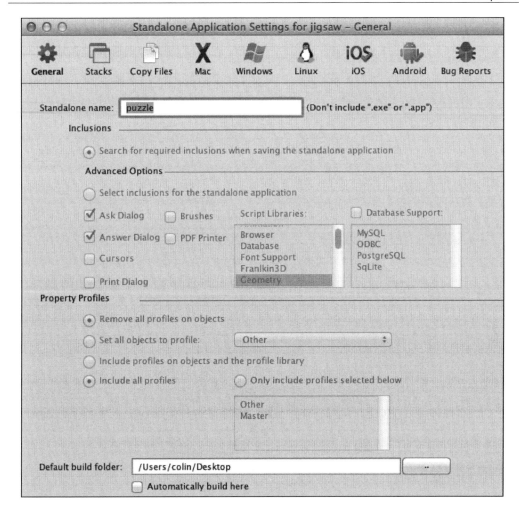

The Stacks section

The **Stacks** section will show you a list of the stacks that are already included in your project. This will of course include the current Mainstack and the stacks that have been added by plugins that you may have used earlier. As you can see, all the options are grayed out.

The Copy Files section

The **Copy Files** section is used to add additional files and folders to be used by your app. These are read-only files; if you need changeable files, you could still include these files and then write copies of the files to the special Documents folder. Here is how the dialog box looks with folders of images and sounds. These folders are in the same folder as the LC app:

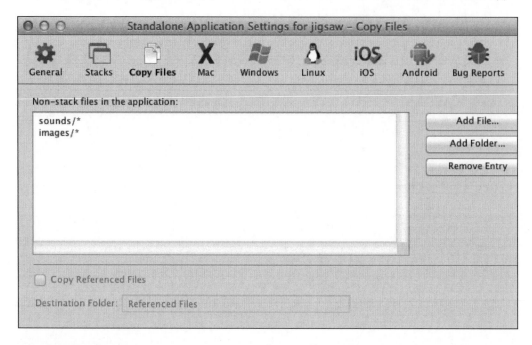

The iOS section

The **Mac**, **Windows**, **Linux**, **Web**, and **Bug Reports** sections are not used while making iOS and Android apps, so now, we'll take a good look at the **iOS** section bit by bit...

The Build for section

The **Build for** settings determine which iOS devices the app will work on and which minimum iOS version should be used. In deciding what to choose, some things are obvious and others, not so obvious. If you are making an app that really needs a large area of workspace, then it might not be too successful on an iPod or iPhone screen. If it's a small utility that is geared for use on a hand-held device, perhaps you don't need to have an iPad version. You are able to choose **iPod**, **iPhone**, and **iPad**, or just **iPod and iPhone**, and even just **iPad** from this section.

The minimum iOS version you choose may depend on the particular features that you have used previously. You don't want users to buy your app only to find that a certain feature doesn't work correctly under the older iOS version. You may need to set and keep some devices for testing to use old versions of the OS on, so that you can be sure that your setting is correct. Also, Xcode allows you to download various versions of Simulator, and in LiveCode, you can choose a specific version to test

You can always leave these options at lower values for now and make up your mind after you have heard how your beta testers get on with the app.

Here is the **Build for** area of the settings along with the menus you can choose from:

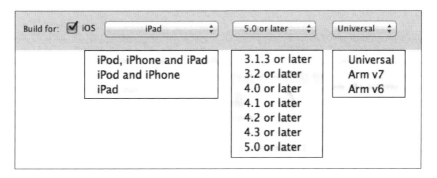

Basic application settings

We have used some of these settings a few times already. Here is the full set of options:

- **Display Name**: This is the name that will appear under the icon on the actual device
- **Version**: This is the version number that will appear in the iTunes description of the app
- **Internal App ID**: This is the app ID that you can use in the iOS Developer portal while developing or distributing the provisioning profile
- **Profile**: This is the provisioning profile that matches this app
- **Externals**: This is a set of optional external command files that you may have used in your app

You should try out different display names to see how it looks on different devices. There is a limit to how long the name can be before iOS truncates the name, placing ellipses in the middle of the text. For iPhone, the limit is roughly up to 11 or 12 characters.

It's important to make sure that an update to an app that you submit has a version number that is later than the version number of the existing app. Starting with 1.0.0 makes sense; just remember to increase the number when you do updates. Don't worry if you forget, you'll find that the upload process to the App Store fails! App stores in general require that the update be of a later version than the one that is being replaced.

For development purposes, you can use a provisioning profile that uses an internal app ID that contains a wildcard. When you do submit an app to iOS App Store, make sure that the provisioning profile is a Distribution one and that the App ID it uses exactly matches the **Internal App ID**. Also, make sure that the ID is different than any other app that you have in the store. Note that the ID, as shown in your developer account page, will show extra digits at its start, for example, `31415926.com.yourname.yourappname`. The matching **Internal App ID** would be `com.yourname.yourappname`.

In this example screenshot, a development provisioning file was chosen and no external commands were used:

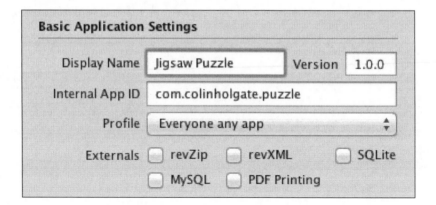

Icons

You are able to select a different icon for each device type that iOS and iTunes requires. The Icons section is straightforward; you click on the ... button and choose the file from your filesystem. It would be possible for LiveCode to take one large image and create the various sizes for you, but there isn't an option for that! For what it's worth, you may have reasons to show a different icon for each case. For example, you could make an icon for Retina displays that had more detail in them than a non-Retina display. As you don't have a choice, just enjoy the flexibility this gives you!

Note the **Prerendered Icon** checkbox in the following screenshot. Here, you have a choice of creating an icon exactly as it should appear on devices. Also, you could produce a square icon with no shading and leave the system to make it look like a button with a highlight effect. Take a look at the various apps on your own devices; you will find that some people were happy to use Apple's beveled highlighted appearance and others preferred to do their own thing. The **Prerendered Icon** feature allows you to do your own thing. In this screenshot, you can see that icons for all the types of devices that have been selected, even iPad Retina, and they are prerendered:

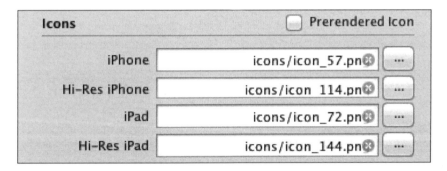

In this case, the `icons/` folder is in the same folder as the app, so you don't need to include the full path. An entry of `icons/` is also included in the **Copy File** section.

A good reference for Apple icon and image sizes for iOS 7+ is available at:

```
https://developer.apple.com/library/ios/documentation/UserExperience/
Conceptual/MobileHIG/IconMatrix.html
```

This chart does not include the old sizes 57 and 72 for the older iPhones and iPads.

Icon tools

There are plenty of tools that will help you create all the icon sizes available in the Mac App Store. When I last checked, there were about 40 icons resulting from a search for `icon ios`. One free tool that I have used is **Icon Set Creator**, which is available at

```
https://itunes.apple.com/us/app/icon-set-creator/id939343785?mt=12
```

Splash screens

Since the very first iPhone, iOS has had the ability to load and show a splash screen immediately when a user touches an app icon. This gives them something to look at while the app loads. All that was needed in those days was a default image and a name `Default.png`. When iPad came along, there became a need for more splash screens. At the very least, you needed a higher resolution default image, but you also needed custom images for landscape, as far as having different landscape images depending on whether the home button is to the left or right.

LiveCode doesn't give us access to that level of flexibility, but it is extremely rare that an app would need a different landscape for two variations; you can generally get by with just a single one. The same for the upside-down portrait variation, the regular default portrait image can be used for that too.

The Retina displays have their own entries for setting the splash screen, and by convention, these files would have names that include `@2x`.

Which of the splash screen options that are enabled is dependent on the orientation options described in the following section. In this screenshot, the **Lscape** options are grayed out because the app is set as **Portrait**. Here, the correct size **Lscape** image files were selected as well, for your reference:

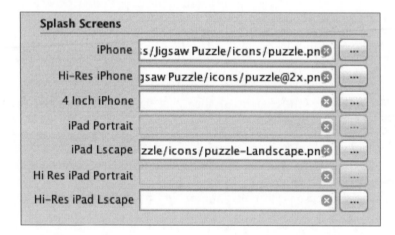

You may notice that there isn't an iPhone portrait or landscape option here. That's because the `Default.png` is used for both. If your app is landscape only, then design the splash screen as landscape, but rotate the image 90 degrees clockwise to create a 320 x 480 or 640 x 960 `Default.png` or `Default@2x.png` image. One important entry in the list is the **4 inch iPhone** entry that is used for iPhone 5. The `Default.png` file name is not used here since image file names can be anything as long as no spaces are included.

Orientation options

As discussed previously, you are able to specify the orientations supported by your app. If the app is used just for iPod and iPhone, then you can set only the initial orientation. The choices are **Portrait**, **Portrait Upside-Down**, **Landscape Left**, and **Landscape Right**. If the app is used on iPad, then you can also set the orientations that support the app while it is in use. The selections you make will affect which icons can be imported. The orientations are all set with just one drop-down menu and four checkboxes:

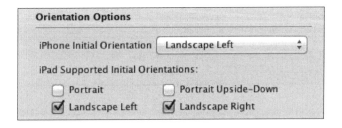

The Custom URL scheme

Sometimes while using an iOS device, you will touch a URL in a web page and suddenly, you will find yourself in Mail or looking at a page in the App Store. This is achieved using a custom URL scheme. In the case of the App Store, links begin with `itms-apps://` and from that iOS knows that the link should be opened in the App Store app. You can do the same thing with your app. By setting a similar custom string, you can get iOS to open your app when the user touches a link that starts with the same string in the URL. Further information can be found in the lesson given at `http://lessons.runrev.com/m/4069/l/58672-using-custom-url-schemes`.

The value of the string is entered with a simple text input field, shown as follows:

Requirements and restrictions

Earlier, we talked about how setting the device, processor instruction set, and iOS version is one way to make sure that your users are able to use the features in your app. The **Requirements and Restrictions** options let you specify in great detail the abilities your device should have. At the very least, if you have an app that involves taking photographs, then having a camera in the device is necessary! If it's a video chat app, then having a front camera in your device would make sense. The reminders app that we made in the previous chapter should have its **Location Services** option selected to make sure that the sort by distance feature works. The following is the full list of requirements and restrictions:

Requirements and Restrictions

☐ Persistent WiFi ☐ File Sharing ☐ Push Notifications

	Required	Prohibited	n/a
Telephony	○	○	⦿
Peer–Peer	○	○	⦿
SMS	○	○	⦿
Still Camera	○	○	⦿
Auto-Focus Camera	○	○	⦿
Front-Facing Camera	○	○	⦿
Camera Flash	○	○	⦿
Video Camera	○	○	⦿
Accelerometer	○	○	⦿
Gyroscope	○	○	⦿
Location Services	○	○	⦿
GPS	○	○	⦿
Magnetometer	○	○	⦿
Microphone	○	○	⦿
Game-Kit	○	○	⦿
WiFi	○	○	⦿
OpenGL ES 1.1	○	○	⦿
OpenGL ES 2.0	○	○	⦿

A status bar

The last option in the iOS settings controls whether the status bar should be visible or not and whether it should have the default status bar appearance or a black appearance. For a black appearance, you can set whether it should be opaque or translucent:

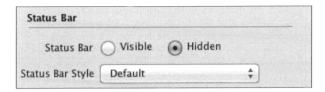

Android

As you'll see, the number of options to be set for Android are less than that for iOS. This isn't so much because Android is simpler, but because LiveCode exposes virtually all of the possible settings for iOS, including a lot that you will most likely not need. iOS also has the splash screen variations that are not available in Android.

In the Android world, there are some settings that you are required to set, in particular, the **Permissions** settings. iOS does ask the user for permission to use some features, but not until the time your app invokes that feature. You must have seen dialog boxes that ask: **Fancy App wants to know your location**. Android on the other hand asks for permission to use these features at the time the app is installed.

Let's look at the options for Android...

Basic application settings

Several of the iOS options are given a different name in the Android OS. Instead of **Display Name**, **Label** is used, **Internal App ID** is called **Identifier**, and there isn't a provisioning file, but there is a **Signing Key** used in Android. Essentially though, they are the same options as in iOS.

The **Icon** is set as part of the basic settings because only one icon is needed, so we don't need a set of options. For this one icon, you would have to select a 512 x 512 sized version of the image and LiveCode will make the other sizes for you.

Android apps don't have a splash screen like iOS, but LiveCode can be given a splash screen that it will show as the first screen that the user sees after the app loads.

You are able to set the location where the app will be installed with choices of **Internal Storage Only**, **Allow External Storage**, and **Prefer External Storage**. The external storage being referred to is the SD memory that most Android devices have. Android users either don't care where the app is installed or they are fanatical about it being stored in the SD memory! You could select **Allow External Storage** and expect a lot of people to do the same or you could choose **Prefer External Storage** knowing that only a minority would change the option to force the installation to be in the internal memory. Overall, you upset less people by using the prefer external storage setting.

In-app purchasing and push notifications are handled in a different way in Android than they are in iOS. If you wish to use in-app purchasing, take a look at the RunRev online lessons and also the `developer.android.com` information. Lessons for Apple, Google, Amazon and Samsung are located at `http://lessons.runrev.com/m/4069`.

The Android developer information on in-app billing can be found at:

`http://developer.android.com/guide/market/billing/billing_overview.html`

As with iOS, an Android OS can be given external commands and it also has the custom URL scheme. One feature that is not found in iOS is the ability to set an icon to be used in the task bar.

Here is how the basic **Application Settings** options are presented:

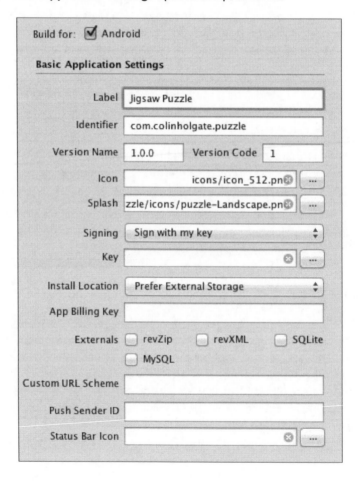

Requirements and restrictions

Within this set of options, you can set the **Minimum Android OS** version and set the hardware features that are required. The columns of radio buttons are named differently in iOS. Instead of stating that a feature is required or prohibited, the buttons state whether the feature is required or used. This becomes information that the Android user is able to read and may play a part in whether they choose to buy your app or not. So, try to select any that can be applied to your app.

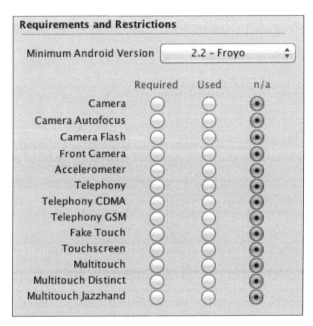

Application permissions

When an iOS app makes use of certain features, such as your location, there is an alert dialog box that appears when the feature is first used. With Android, any such features are listed during the installation of the app and the user gives permission for all the features in one go.

Here is the list of permissions you can choose from:

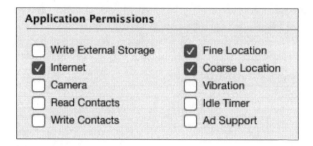

User interface options

User Interface Options perform the same function as the orientation and status bar options in iOS. If you are submitting an iPad app that is landscape, you have to support both variations of landscape. The Android app stores don't have the same requirement, so the options are much simpler. You only have to choose whether the initial orientation should be **Portrait** or **Landscape** and whether the status bar should be **Visible** or **Hidden**:

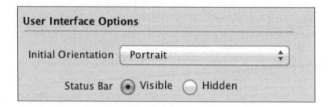

Building Apps for Beta Testers

You may have given test builds to friends and colleagues all the way through the process of developing your app, but even if you haven't, it becomes more important to do so as you get closer to the time when you have to upload the app to the app stores. Beta testers can tell you about technical and nontechnical issues. Are there any typos in the Credits? Does the icon look good? Were there any strange aspects to the installation experience? And of course, does the app do what it's supposed to do on the numerous devices and OSes?

The process of making an app to send it to a tester is different on Android than on iOS. In fact, it's incredibly easy on Android! Let's look at that first.

Sending an Android app to testers

When click on the **Save as Standalone Application...** option for Android, you create an *APK* file. You could e-mail this file to your testers and they could do what is called a "side load" of the file on their device. In *Chapter 2, Getting Started with LiveCode Mobile*, we saw how tricky it can be to connect an Android device for testing and it could well be beyond the technical abilities of some of your testers.

Fortunately, there is a much simpler approach to do this. Take the APK file and put it online somewhere. It can be on a Dropbox shared location, Google Drive, or perhaps just a server at your office. Whatever it takes for you to get to the point where you have a URL that has a link to the file. Now e-mail that URL to your testers to an e-mail address that they can read on their devices. Then, it only takes a single touch of the link in the e-mail for you to start the download and installation of your app.

There is a Development section in the Android device settings that the testers may need to visit to enable the feature that allows apps to be installed in this way, but it's very easy to make this change.

Preparing an iOS app so that it can work on someone else's device

Things are not quite as straightforward for iOS! First thing you need to do is add the unique device ID (UDID) for each of your beta testers' devices to your iOS developer account. Your testers can get that number by connecting the device to their computer and viewing its Info in iTunes. When you're looking at the **Summary** section, you will see the serial number for the respective device. Clicking on that number will make it change to a longer number, the UDID that will be needed. Once that number is displayed, you can use a keyboard shortcut to copy the number to the clipboard (*command* + *C* on Mac and *Ctrl* + *C* on Windows). Have your testers perform these actions and then paste the number in an e-mail to you. You must make sure that you get the number right because it will use up one of your 100 allocated devices of your iOS developer account.

Go to `https://developer.apple.com/account/ios/device/deviceList.action` in order to add the devices to your account. Click on the **+** button just below the place where your name appears and you will be able to add the devices to your account:

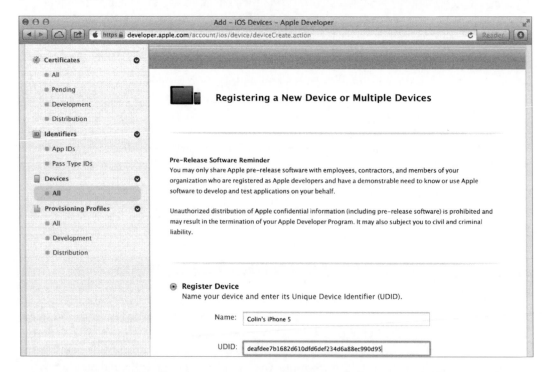

Next, go to the **Provisioning Profiles** section and either create a new **Development** profile or select an existing one and click on the **Edit** button. After selecting an App ID and a signing certificate, you will then see a list of the devices associated with your account. You can enable any combination of devices you want to work with this provisioning profile. In this screenshot, you'll see that the pool of test devices is very short:

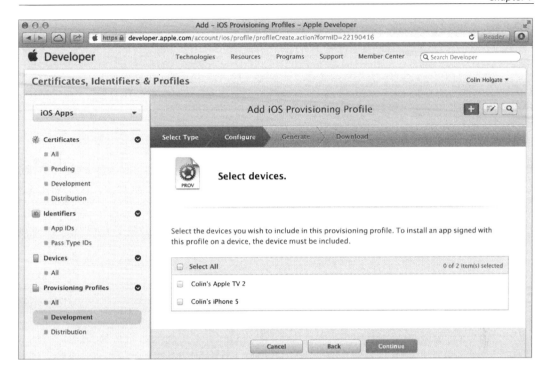

Click on the **Generate** button and after a few moments, you will be able to click on the **Download** button to download the file.

Download the new profile and add it to Xcode (just double click on the downloaded file). Open your app's Mainstack in LiveCode, go to **Standalone Application Settings…/iOS**, and make sure that the provisioning profile is selected from the **Profile** menu. Click on the **Save as Standalone Application…** option again to make sure that the new devices are known by the app.

By now, you will have an "APP" file, which is the iOS equivalent of the "APK" file for Android. As with Android, you could e-mail this file to your testers along with the provisioning file and have the testers "side load" it onto their devices. In this instance, that's not such a difficult task because the tester can use iTunes to do the same. If you do go down that route, have your testers drag the "APP" and provisioning files onto the **Library** in iTunes, connect the device, view the **Apps** tab, make sure that the new app is selected, and perform a **Sync**. However, it is possible to make things a lot easier for your users, as easy as they were for Android users.

Using "over the air" installers for iOS

Since iOS 4.0, it has been possible for us to install an app from a link in a web page. Creating the file structure for this to work is a bit tricky though, but fortunately, there are at least a couple of tools you can buy to make things easy for you.

AirLaunch

HyperActive Software has made a LiveCode plugin that can take your "APP" file and make the file structure needed for the "over the air" installation to work. There is just a single dialog box that you need to fill the required information in:

After selecting the "APP" file, you only need to enter the URL where the folder will be when it's online and then click on the **Create Files** button. The URL link to your online app will be confirmed at the bottom of the window. Click on the URL to copy it and then e-mail it to your testers. When they visit the web page on their device, there will be a single link to touch and iOS will prompt you for approval to install the app. If you look at the next available position on your home page, you will see that it is being installed or is already installed if you are not quick enough.

 For more information about AirLaunch, refer to:
`http://www.hyperactivesw.com/airlaunch/index.html`

Note that Apple requires a secure server for this to work and the URL must start with HTTPS. The easiest source is to use a Dropbox public folder, though you need to make it secure if you've signed up for Dropbox after October 4, 2012. Refer to the AirLaunch FAQs for further information at:

`http://hyperactivesw.com/airlaunch/airlaunchtips.html`

 AirLaunch workflow in development

AirLaunch can be installed as a LiveCode plugin and can be run right after you create a standalone version of your app. You can save the installation web page on your iOS device and click on it to launch the installer. This method is a lot easier to test your app during development than connecting a cable to your device and dragging the app into Xcode.

BetaBuilder

BetaBuilder can be found in the Mac App Store at:

`http://itunes.apple.com/us/app/betabuilder-for-ios-apps/`
`id415348946?mt=12`

It wasn't made with LiveCode in mind and works with "IPA" files and not "APP" files. An easy way to convert the LiveCode APP file into an IPA file is to drag the APP file into iTunes and to select Show in Finder by right-clicking on the app in the **Library**. This will reveal the IPA file that you can drag into the BetaBuilder window.

The process is much the same as AirLaunch's process, where you select the file to use, enter the URL of the online folder, and the program generates the files for you. Again, this all happens in a single dialog window:

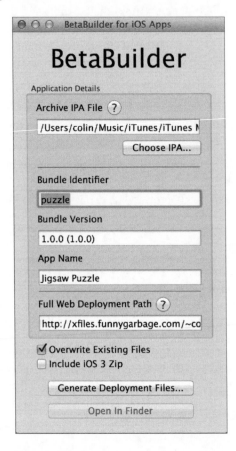

Both products create similar files as illustrated in the following Dropbox public folder:

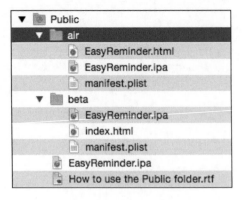

Both products make life easy for your testers. AirLaunch has the advantages of being a plugin that works within LiveCode, which you're likely to have open anyway, and working directly with the APP files that LiveCode creates. BetaBuilder is a Mac app that is run separately and requires you to transfer the files to your server using some other Mac application. AirTouch has FTP built-in to streamline your workflow.

BetaBuilder's main advantage is that it's incredibly cheap! It also generates a web page that is more informative than AirLaunch, which shows just a simple link with the name of the app. However, AirLaunch allows you to export the template and edit or integrate it into your website.

Install Link

Tap Here to Install
EasyReminder 1.0.0 (1.0.0)
Directly On Your Device

Link didn't work?
Make sure you're visiting this page on your device,
not your computer.

Last Updated: Jan 26, 2015

Created With BetaBuilder for iOS Apps

TestFlight

A service named TestFlight was in place during the time I was writing the first edition of this book that worked similar to AirLaunch and Beta Builder. In 2014, Apple purchased TestFlight and merged it with **iTunes Connect (iTC)** that is used to submit apps to the Apple App Store. TestFlight is a lot more than what you need to just send out personal apps to a few testers, but it is required while dealing with apps that go out to as many as 1000 testers. One big change is that you will also need a Distribution Profile and Certificate to start the submittal process as described further in this chapter.

TestFlight has two levels of testing: **Internal** and **External**. Internal testing is for members of your development team. You can add up to 25 internal testers using the **Users and Roles** section of iTC and assign them a **Technical** role. They will get an e-mail invitation and need to activate an iTC account. When you start testing your app, they receive another e-mail announcement and need to download the TestFlight app to their device that must run iOS 8 or its later versions. The TestFlight app then installs your app for testing. The test only lasts for 30 days unless you update it and submit a new version. The TestFlight app can also be used for error reporting and feedback.

External testing is similar, but requires a Beta App Review and must comply with the full App Store Review Guidelines before the testing begins. A review is required for new versions of your app that contain significant changes. Up to 10 apps can be tested at a time, internally or externally. You can add up to 1000 external testers just by supplying a list of their e-mail addresses and checking whether you have their approval. After releasing, the testing proceeds in the same manner as it did with internal testers. At the time of writing this book, a tester could not be on both the internal and external lists. Refer to `https://developer.apple.com/testflight/` for further information.

Missing push notification entitlement

In early 2015, you would get this e-mail warning message while submitting an app to iTC: "Your app appears to include API used to register with the Apple **Push Notification** service, but the app signature's **entitlements** do not include the "aps-environment" **entitlement**." This is an issue in LC and does not affect anything. Apple's Push Notification Service is built in the LC engine and LC doesn't bother to strip it out if you don't use it. It is documented in bug 10979 in the RunRev Quality system at `http://quality.runrev.com/process_bug.cgi`.

Using "over the air" installers for Android

While testing with the Android Emulator or direct connection should be sufficient to learn LiveCode development, the real world is much more complex. In the last several years, testing alternatives have emerged to help test your apps on other Android devices. With numerous Android devices, this is really needed. There were 8614 listed in the Google Play store at the last count and many more must've been listed even now, when you read this. There are also variations in the Android OS available at Amazon, Samsung, and others. Hopefully, testing through Google testing resources will be adequate for your needs.

Google testing

Google also has a testing capability built in their Google Play store. As with Apple's iTC and TestFlight; for Google, you have to prepare your store list and upload your APK just as you would when publishing it. To distribute to testers, you need to create and select a Google Group or Google+ Community that the testers join. Google has alpha and beta tests, which are similar to Apple's internal and external testing. Notification e-mails are sent to testers with a link to the testing section of Google Play. Because your testers can't leave public reviews for alpha/beta apps on Google Play, it's a good idea to let them know where they can provide you feedback (an e-mail address, website, and so on). Further details can be found at:

`https://support.google.com/googleplay/android-developer/answer/3131213?hl=en`

Amazon testing

Amazon has a tool called **Live App Testing** to allow developers to beta test apps through the Amazon appstore. Developers can invite up to 500 specific users to test the app through an e-mail invite. In addition to this, the **A/B Testing Service** allows to conduct in-app experiments to try different UI interactions with different groups of users. It supposedly also supports iOS, but requires specific APIs that would need development of LiveCode externals.

For more information refer to:

```
https://developer.amazon.com/public/community/post/TxCVSAM1IG7NX2/
Launch-Better-Apps-Announcing-Live-App-Testing
```

Samsung testing

To facilitate testing of apps, Samsung has developed **Remote Testing Lab (RTL)** facilities. These labs contain real devices that allow developers to upload and test their apps. To use these devices, you need to download and run a Java applet that connects your APK to a live device in the Samsung lab and provides an interface to interact with this device. This may have some potential in the future, but is included here for possible investigation. For more information on Samsung testing, refer to `http://developer.samsung.com/remotetestlab/rtlAboutRTL.action`.

The previous testing alternatives are the primary alternatives associated with the iOS and Android device manufacturers. Since Apple bought **TestFlight**, several other cross-platform testing solutions have picked up the slack. A quick search on the Internet shows **HockeyApp**, **Crashlytics**, **Ubertesters**, **TestFairy**, and others that may have potential as well.

Creating an app store submission file

The biggest hurdle 'that you need to overcome in order to make a version of your app that can be submitted to app stores is acquiring a distribution certificate. The process is quicker for Android, but does involve some typing to be done in the command line, and there is a slight difference if you are on Windows rather than Mac. The iOS process has many steps to it, but at least they don't involve typing cryptic commands. We'll look at Android first.

Finding and using the Android Keytool application

One of the thing that was installed when you added the Java Development Kit is a tool to make a "keystore" file, which is a self-assigned certificate. It's this tool that is used to create the certificate you'll need in order to distribute an Android app.

On Mac, you don't need to find this application, you can simply type the command in the Terminal and you'll find the tool. On Windows, you need to navigate to the folder where Keytool is located first. Before getting that far, you have to first open the command line as Administrator.

On Windows, the CMD application is found at `C:\Windows\System32\`. Go to that directory in Windows Explorer, right-click on the file, and select **Run as Administrator**. The Keytool application will be in the bin folder of the Java JDK directory. Once you are at Command Prompt, change directories to get to that location, which will be something like `C:\Program Files\Java\jdkx.x.x_xx\bin\`, where the `jdkx.x.x_xx` part would actually be the version of the JDK that you have installed. You should be able to get all the way there with a line like the following, where cd is the command used to change directories:

```
C:\> cd \Program Files\Java\jdk1.7.0_01\bin\
```

On Mac, you will use Terminal, which is located in `/Application/Utilites`. Just open Terminal and you'll immediately be able to use the Keytool application.

In either case, you will now type a relatively short line and then answer the various questions that appear. For better understanding of what is going on, visit:

`http://developer.android.com/guide/publishing/app-signing.html`

For our purpose, we'll just type in the right command, and all should go well, even if we don't understand what we typed!

This is the line that you need to type, changing the keystore and alias names to match the names you wish to use for this certificate:

```
keytool -genkey -v -keystore my-release-key.keystore
-alias alias_name -keyalg RSA -keysize 2048 -validity 10000
```

When you press the Enter or Return key, you will start to see a series of questions starting with the password you wish to use for the keystore. Further questions will ask for your full name, details about your company, city, and country. It's a set of data that can be encoded into a keystore that is unique and has enough accurate information through which a user can decide whether to trust the certificate.

When the tool is finished, you will have the keystore file that LiveCode requires. It will be easily available in your home folder on Mac and somewhat buried in the JDK bin folder on Windows.

Go to the **Basic Application Settings** of the **Standalone Application Settings** of your Mainstack and navigate to the file from the Key entry. Once chosen, this section will look like this:

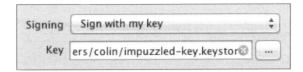

If you have chosen your icons and splash screen and requirements and permissions, you should be able to build a version of the APK file that can be uploaded to app stores.

Creating a distribution certificate for iOS

As mentioned previously, there is no command line typing involved to get a distribution certificate for iOS, but there are a lot of steps involved. The First place to visit to get the certificate is the iOS Developer Portal to make sure that you have set up a dedicated App ID and Provisioning file for this particular app.

The following screenshot represents the steps taken to get a certificate and profile for an app that is to be named `EasyReminder`, which is the reminder app that we made earlier.

In the **App IDs** part of the portal, there is a **+** button that adds a new app ID to your account and asks for a name for that ID. Here, you can see that the ID is given the name **EasyReminder** and a Bundle Identifier `com.gerdeen.easyreminder`. This needs to match the **Internal App ID** set in LiveCode. If you are *not* member of multiple development teams, you will not see the App ID Prefix shown in the following screenshot:

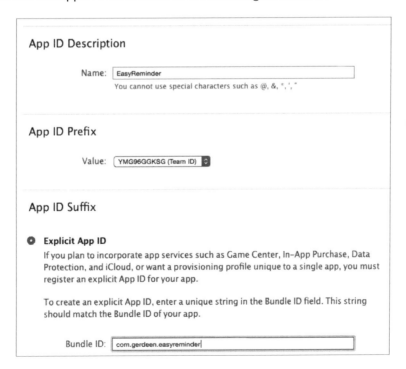

Now that there is an App ID, it can be used to set up a Distribution Provisioning Profile in the **Provisioning** section. If you haven't yet made a Distribution Certificate, you will see a button telling you to make one. Clicking on that button will present you a question about what kind of certificate you want to make:

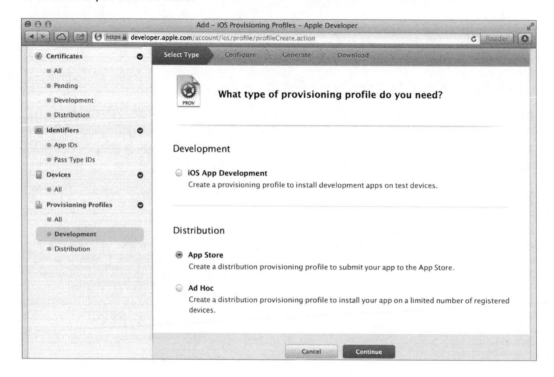

Clicking on the **Continue** button takes you to a long description of how you have to make a request to the certificate authority and how to upload a file that Keychain Access generates. When you encounter this situation, carefully follow the steps shown in the following screenshot:

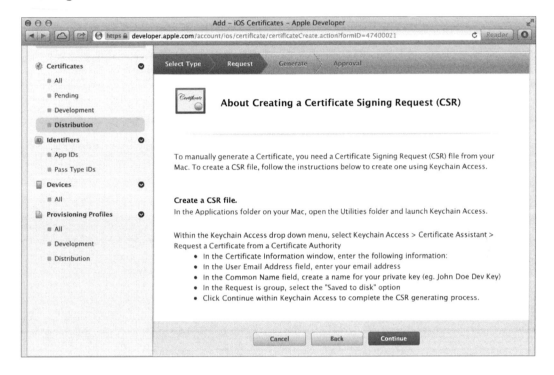

After you have uploaded that certificate request file, you will be able to make a distribution profile that uses the dedicated App ID and the distribution certificate. The final entry will look like this, and you can use the **Download** button to get a local copy of the provisioning file:

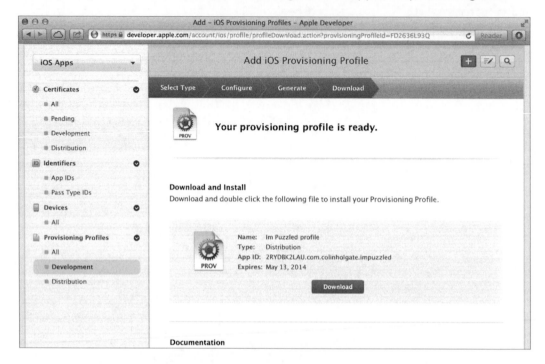

You now have the file that LiveCode requires, only you don't select it in the LiveCode settings. Instead, you double-click on the file and it installs itself using Xcode. Once it is in Xcode, you can then select it from the **Profile** menu in the **Basic Application Settings** in LiveCode:

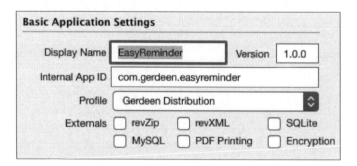

As with Android, make sure to add icons, splash screens, set requirements, and so on and you will be able to save an APP file, ready to go, to the iOS App Store.

Uploading to the app stores

Each app store guides you through the steps of how to upload a new app and there are quite a lot of steps involved! It could take another book to show you all the screenshots you have to wade through. Showing these screenshots here would not be so valuable mainly because of their large quantity, but also because the process changes from time to time. For example, Google changed the name of their service from Android Market to Google Play.

There is some similarity between what each of the stores asks you, so we'll look at what preparations you might need before heading off to the stores. When you are ready to proceed with the uploading, these are the pages you need to start with for the respective app stores:

- iTunes Connect: `https://itunesconnect.apple.com`
- Google Play: `https://play.google.com/apps/publish/`
- Amazon Appstore: `https://developer.amazon.com/home.html`
- Samsung Apps: `https://seller.samsungapps.com/`

What's similar

All three app stores will ask for a description of what the app does, rating information, price, a support website or e-mail address, and category information. In order to ask a price, other than Free, you will have to set up a merchant account. In the case of Apple, you'll have to give a web page address for support. Google just asks for contact information and Amazon shows support as being optional. All three ask for screenshots and allow you to upload a demo video.

What's different

Apple asks for a lot of information, but spread over many screens. As you enter data, you will need screenshots and other information that you haven't gathered. You can **Save** what you have entered and come back later. Be sure to get it right before you click on **Submit for Review** because Apple does not allow you to change the information without uploading a newer version of the app.

The upload of the actual app file for iOS is handled by the Application Loader utility that comes as part of Xcode. To access Application Loader from the Xcode developer tools package, choose menu **Xcode | Open Developer Tool | Application Loader**. You can also download it in your Application folder as described in the iTunes Connect support document at:

`https://itunesconnect.apple.com/docs/UsingApplicationLoader.pdf`

Google asks for a lot of information, but it's all in their Developer Console. There are sections for uploading the **APK**, for completing the **Store Listing** and **Pricing & Distribution** as well as other operations. Be careful if you set the price as free as you cannot change it and it's instantly and permanently declared a free app. To change it later, you would need to create a new app with a new package name and set a price for the new app.

Amazon asks for about the same information as Apple and Google. You can check whether your app works with Amazon by simply dragging it to their developer web page. They run a quick compatibility test and then run more tests on Android Nexus 7 and their Fire phones and tablets. You can start the submittal process for your app directly from the test results page, but then you need to establish a developer account and provide the same information as before.

Samsung Apps is an app store designed to provide apps specially customized for Samsung mobile phones. It is a focal point for both developers and Samsung handset users. Without actually signing up, it is difficult to get details of how the store works for non-Samsung devices. For additional information, review the article at `http://www.pivoteast.com/guide-how-to-register-and-submit-apps-to-samsung-apps/`.

Bottom line

The submission process is just about the most stressful part of developing a mobile app! It makes you feel better about the other stages you've been through; perhaps those weren't so bad after all...

Hopefully, you have a partner who can be a second pair of eyes to help you understand all the questions to not miss something vital that will haunt you later.

Summary

I don't know about you, but I'm beat! This mobile app developing business can be overwhelming. Even the administrative side of things can be quite involved. In this chapter, we covered some of the less programmatic tasks such as examining all the options in the Standalone Application Settings, fighting our way through command lines and red tape to get an app certified, and mentally preparing ourselves to submit our app to app stores.

We're at the end of the road as far as making use of mobile features in a LiveCode stack and taking them through to the point of making a real mobile app out of them is concerned. Next up, we'll look at a few add-ons to LiveCode that would enable you to use even more mobile features.

Extending LiveCode

The story so far...

"The Long and Winding Road" was the last single to be released by the Beatles and it would make a good title for a book describing what it took to get LiveCode working on mobile devices! As soon as there were apps on iPhone, RunRev was developing a way to publish apps on iPhone from LiveCode. Then, in April 2010, Steve Jobs wrote this infamous article on Flash, which you can find at:

```
http://www.apple.com/hotnews/thoughts-on-flash/
```

Adobe was also developing a way to publish apps on iPhone from Flash Professional, but as part of Apple's determination to not allow Flash-based apps to be usable on iPhone, the App Store submission rules were changed, forbidding developers from using any tool other than Xcode to publish apps.

Some tools continued to be in a gray area because they used Xcode to do the final publishing. GameSalad and Unity apps continued to be published and did well in the App Store. RunRev tried to convince Apple to allow LiveCode (which was still called **Runtime Revolution** at the time) as a publishing tool for iPhone, even promising to only publish apps on iPhone and to not pursue publishing on Android. Apple stood its ground and declined the offer.

For Adobe, this wasn't the end of the world and it started working on Android publishing. However, RunRev had already planned a conference around the idea of publishing apps to iOS, but that conference had to be postponed.

During the summer of 2010, Apple ran a survey for developers and several of the questions mentioned in it gave people like me a chance to beg Apple to allow developers to use their preferred development tools so that they don't have a compulsion to use Xcode. It's hard to be sure whether that's what made the difference, but on September 9, 2010, Apple changed its position on the subject. Here is the post that we woke up to that morning:

```
http://www.apple.com/pr/library/2010/09/09Statement-by-Apple-on-App-
Store-Review-Guidelines.html
```

Colin Holgate (coauthor of this book) quickly posted a message to the Revolution e-mail list titled "*how to totally make Kevin's day*"; "Kevin" being Kevin Miller, the CEO of RunRev. It had the desired effect and you can still read the follow up messages at:

```
http://runtime-revolution.278305.n4.nabble.com/how-to-totally-make-
Kevin-s-day-td2532866.html
```

This got RunRev back on track to achieve its goal of developing a "Publish to iOS" feature; The iPhone OS was renamed as iOS by that time. The delayed conference ended up taking place in San Jose at the end of April 2011. By that time, RunRev had not only made the iOS feature work well, but it had also released the first version of the "Publish to Android" feature.

It's quite amusing in a way to think that if you intend to publish an app on Android from LiveCode, you can thank Apple for being so stubborn!

Extending LiveCode

The progress on LiveCode continued at quite a fast pace and by April 2012, RunRev had implemented all the iOS features for Android as well as added a lot to the feature set for iOS.

Still today, not every feature is covered and there is a third-party market of add-ons to LiveCode, which either makes developing in LiveCode easier or provide features that are not yet available in the standard version. Here are some of the add-ons, most of which can be bought from the LiveCode Marketplace at:

```
http://www.runrev.com/store/
```

MobGUI

We already used **MobGUI** in earlier chapters. It takes the form of a plugin. You can place the MobGUI file in your `plugins` folder. The LiveCode lesson at `http://lessons.runrev.com/s/lessons/m/4071/l/21341-how-to-install-custom-user-plugins` describes how to add plugins.

The way MobGUI works is that it lets you place the regular LiveCode controls onto your stack's card and then when the app is run, the standard controls are swapped for native controls. This has an advantage over just making standard controls that look like iOS controls, because the control will look correct too.

MobGUI doesn't do anything that you cannot do with your own scripts, but it does make it a lot easier to lay out and use mobile OS native controls. It has an option to switch between iOS and Android themes. There is a YouTube channel for MobGUI that will show you some of the things that can be done using the tool, which you can find at:

`http://www.youtube.com/user/MobGUI`

tmControl

The **tmControl** is a set of themes made by **Tactile Media** that lets you give your LiveCode stacks a more artistic appearance. In addition to sci-fi and other themes, there is an iOS theme that you can find in `tmControl`. Here's what it looks like:

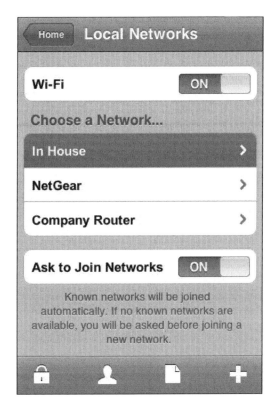

Not too surprising really! An Android theme is planned as well as additions to the iOS theme. You can find the currently available themes at:

`http://tmtools.tactilemedia.com/tmcontrol/themes.html`

The DropTools palette

Made by Sons of Thunder Software, the DropTools Palette is a free add-on to LiveCode, which acts as a shell to host many types of custom LiveCode controls. In addition to being the holder for Sons of Thunder custom controls, it is also used by other developers as an easy way to bring their own custom controls to market. The DropTools website includes detailed descriptions of how you can develop your own DropTools compatible controls.

The site also acts as an *aggregator* for custom LiveCode controls and includes links to both DropTools and non-DropTools compatible add-ons. The main page of DropTools is located at:

`http://droptools.sonsothunder.com/`

Many of the custom controls do not relate to mobile apps, but there are a few that do and that number will no doubt increase over time. DropTools does not work with the Community version of LiveCode, though they are trying to reverse the situation.

mergExt

The `mergExt` extension is a suite of external commands for LiveCode. At the time of writing this book, there was no LiveCode Android SDK available, so currently, these are all only for iOS. Here is the list, as it stands, along with the description taken from the LiveCode Marketplace page `http://mergext.com`:

- `mergAccessory`: This is an iOS external used to connect to and communicate with accessory hardware using the **External Accessory framework**.

- `mergAES`: This provides easy-to-use AES 128 and 256 encryption in the CBC or ECB mode.

- `mergAnswerColor`: This is an iOS external that presents a modal color picker.

- `mergAV`: This is an iOS external that adds functions and commands related to the **AVFoundation framework**. This currently includes selecting, recording, saving, and editing videos.

- `mergAWS`: This is an iOS and MacOS X external that adds functions and commands to use Amazon web services.

- `mergBanner`: This is an iOS external that adds an **iAd banner** to your app at the bottom of the screen.

♦ `mergBgTask`: This is an iOS external that adds commands to start and stop background tasks on iOS. Background tasks allow your app to continue executing the code while in the background.

♦ `mergBonjour`: This is an iOS external that implements the bonjour service; searching and registration.

♦ `mergCL`: This implements significant location change and region monitoring. The external will allow iOS to wake your app up in the background and receive a message when the user enters or exits a region or moves a significant distance.

♦ `mergDoc`: This is an iOS external that adds functions and commands related to document interaction. This currently includes presenting a modal preview, opening in app menu, document options menu, and requesting the document icons in PNG form. Printing is also available here via the preview.

♦ `mergDropbox`: This is an iOS external used to interact with a user's Dropbox account. The external enables you to upload and download files, create folders, and manage the files on the user's Dropbox account.

The Dropbox Sync SDK handles all the syncing of files for you and allows you to interact with your app directory just like a local filesystem.

♦ `mergFTPD`: This adds an FTP daemon to your app allowing FTP client connections. Use `mergFTPD` to manage your app's files from your desktop version

♦ `mergGK`: This is an iOS external that adds GameKit/Game Center commands and functions to LiveCode.

♦ `mergJSON`: This is a JSON encoding/decoding external that supports all the platforms LiveCode supports.

♦ `mergLA`: This is an iOS external that adds a command to present a local authentication dialog box to the user if they have set up the biometric touch ID authentication.

♦ `mergMKs`: This is a LiveCode MapKit external that adds a map control, which supports and shows the user's location with a heading, adding annotation pins, and polylines.

♦ `mergMP`: This is an iOS external that adds functions and commands related to the MediaPlayer framework. This currently includes functions such as querying the iPod library and accessing the properties of the found media collections.

♦ `mergNIC`: This is an iOS external used to obtain information about the network interfaces active on the device.

♦ `mergNotify`: This is an iOS external that adds a command to request a notification callback whenever the iOS Notification Center receives the event notification.

♦ `mergPop`: This is an iOS external that adds functions to present an action sheet (pop over on an iPad) and contextual menu for user interaction.

- `mergReader`: This is an iOS external that presents a modal PDF reader using the open source `vfrReader` project.

- `mergSettings`: This is an iOS external that integrates a LiveCode app with the **Settings** app and also includes `InAppSettingsKit` to present a matching dialog box from within your app.

- `mergSocial`: This is an iOS external that adds commands to present Twitter, Facebook, and Weibo post modal views.

- `mergSocket`: This is an iOS external that provides TCP and UDP (datagram) client and server sockets.

- `mergXattr`: This is an iOS external that adds commands to set the `do not backup` and `protection` attributes of a file.

- `mergZXing`: This is a LiveCode external that uses the `ZXing` library to read a wide range of barcode types via the rear camera of a mobile device.

animationEngine

This allows you to create smooth animations and detect collisions between objects. It is well suited for both creating games and making presentation apps. You can find its information page at the LiveCode Marketplace website `https://livecode.com/store/marketplace/animation-engine-5/`.

Although not specifically for mobile use, `animationEngine` has been adjusted to comply with iOS App Store requirements and so it should still be of use to make iOS apps. It also works for Android apps.

AirLaunch

As shown in the *Creating over the air installers for iOS* section in the last chapter, AirLaunch is an add-on that makes it easy to create over-the-air installer files for iOS. A detailed description for this can be found at:

`http://www.hyperactivesw.com/airlaunch/index.html`

The ControlManager IDE

ControlManager from The Flexible Learning Company is an IDE palette designed to provide easy-view access to your project's structure, properties, and layout. It is compatible with the free edition of LiveCode as well as the commercial edition for Windows, Mac, and Linux platforms. It keeps up with your actions in the IDE and updates itself as you work.

ControlManager has three tab displays designed to support the IDE that present structure, properties, and geometry as an easy-to-use overview.

- ◆ **Control Browser**: This is a navigable structural hierarchy with shuffle options and control-specific icon identification from deeply nested groups up to an overview of all available stacks, subStacks, and cards.

- ◆ **Property Editor**: This allows you to preview, compare, and edit any property for any control, group, card, subStack, or stack in one easy-to-see list. These can be listed alphabetically or by type, including access to basic or multidimensional custom properties. You can apply any visual effect from `dropShadows` to `colorOverlays` with built-in drag controls for `fillGradient` and `strokeGradient`.

- ◆ **Geometry Editor**: This contains point-and-click features for 3-way resizing, 4-way nudging, 9-way alignment, 6-way distribution, and 5-way layering with 7 image manipulation options. Using LiveCode's frontscript layer, the palette keeps up with you automatically, refreshing as you shuffle between objects, cards, and stacks. For more information regarding ControlManager, refer to `http://www.flexiblelearning.com/controlmanager/`.

Creating your own add-ons

The two main types of add-ons that you might be interested in making are custom controls and external commands and functions (generally referred to as **externals**).

Custom controls

Custom controls are typically made of a group that holds many standard controls and a group script that manages the appearance and interactions of these controls. A custom control's functionality is entirely encapsulated within itself and doesn't affect its environment in any way. There is a tutorial on how to make such a custom control at:

`http://lessons.runrev.com/m/4071/l/22272-custom-controls`

If you intend to go on to make a nice custom palette, to make it easy to drag-and-drop your custom controls onto the card window, consider making it DropTools compatible. You would save yourself a significant amount of time solving the issue that DropTools already solves, and your custom controls would fit in with the other DropTools controls, making the screen less crowded with custom palettes! There is a lot of information available on how to develop DropTools compatible controls at:

`http://droptools.sonsothunder.com/developer/`

Externals

Down the left-hand side of the previously-mentioned "lessons" page is a long list of tutorials, several of which relate to the topic of making externals. These particular tutorials are intended to develop externals for desktop applications. To develop mobile externals, you should check out:

```
http://livecode.com/developers/guides/externals/
```

At the time of writing, this page only covers iOS externals, but there is reason to hope that by the time you read this book, there will be information on how to create Android externals too. This page is quite long and even includes a 17-minute video! The video can also be viewed on YouTube at:

```
https://www.youtube.com/watch?feature=player_embedded&v=lqduyQkhigg
```

Creating externals is not simple. If you have an idea for a useful external, but feel it's beyond your abilities or interest to create, take a look at the mergExt site:

```
http://mergext.com
```

Here, you can make suggestions for externals that you would like to see created.

If you do feel you can make externals, why not make them available as products? The going rate for these add-ons is in the $30-$100 range—any sales you make will offset your development costs.

Open source

LiveCode Community is an Open Source application. This means that you can look at and edit all of the code used to run it, including the engine code.

Any apps you create using LiveCode Community must be open source. You can sell what you make, but you must make your source code public under the GPL license. You can include it with your distributed app or include a link to it that users can click on to view your code. If at any time you want to create a professional app and protect your code, you can purchase a Commercial license for LiveCode, which allows you to build a closed source app.

If you know C++, you can get right into the code and add your own features, fixes, and enhancements. After a screening process, your new features can get incorporated into LiveCode itself, making it better for everybody. The following link shows you how you can contribute to the effort:

```
http://livecode.com/community/contribute-to-livecode/
```

Users wishing to contribute code are required to sign a contributor's agreement that can be found at:

`http://livecode.com/store/account/contributor-agreement-signup`

RunRev uses **GitHub** to host the source files that make up LiveCode. This is where all the interaction with the LiveCode source files takes place. If you want to make changes to LiveCode, you will need a GitHub account and understand how to use it. If you are only interested in obtaining an open source copy of the LiveCode files, you can download the zipped bundle from GitHub without having to register at `https://github.com/runrev/livecode`.

Quality control

If you are not comfortable working with C++ and you've come across a bug, you can report it and request features in the traditional way. You can help RunRev improve the quality of LiveCode by getting involved in the bug management process. In particular, there is ample opportunity for you to help reproduce reported bugs and fix bugs in the source code.

The **Quality Control Center** is open to everyone. You can report bugs, request that bugs are assigned to you, and watch the progress of bugs that are being addressed. A helpful search bar is provided at the bottom of your Quality Control Center screen. This gives you access to bugs that you raised, that are assigned to you, that require investigation, and fixes that are ready for the next release. You can create your own Quality Control Center account by going to:

`http://quality.runrev.com/`

Once you have set up an account, you can continue to use this link to access the Quality Control Center in the future. You should search the database for similar problems before submitting a new bug.

A New World of Extensions

Up to this point in time of writing, everything that we've discussed is available. However, there is a new world coming in the LiveCode 8.0 development. The following text is a look at the future as presented at the RunRev14 conference in September 2014 and as presented in an early 2015 newsletter status report by Benjamin Beaumont of LiveCode. We have been hearing about an **Open Language** and **Widgets**. Some of the terminology and details may change from what we present here. Indeed, Open Language already has seen the terms of LiveCodish, Modular LiveCode, and now LiveCode Builder.

While all the previous add-ons were extensions, the term is taking on an expanded meaning. An extension is a black box that extends the engine in some way, exporting handlers that perform specific functions. They are insulated from the rest of the engine and each other.

The new **Extensions** can be libraries or widgets. Libraries are the replacement for externals, add commands, and functions that are like the built-in ones and are not in the message path. Parameters can be typed, eliminating the need for repetitive type checking of the code. They also support seamless usage of foreign code. Libraries are written in exactly the same way as a widget except that any "public" handlers in the library are made available as syntax in the LiveCode Script.

A **Widget** in LiveCode is a script that has direct access to the 2D drawing library and a canvas to draw on. Widgets are like existing built-in controls that you select from the tools palette. In particular, widgets have complete control over how they respond and which messages the LiveCode script sees.

Widgets are implemented as a collection of event handlers, such as `mouseEnter`, `mouseLeave`, `mouseMove`, `mouseDown`, `mouseUp`, `mouseRelease`, `keyPress`, `save`, `load`, and finally `paint`. The `paint` event is called to render a widget using 2D canvas syntax. All operations use floating point coordinates, so we will have subpixel positioning. Widgets will be able to have a tree of child widgets internally, so that complex widgets can be built out of simple widgets.

Inside extensions

Extensions are built and distributed as single file archives that contain a compiled LiveCode Builder, the original LiveCode Builder source (nonoptional if an open source extension!), compiled foreign code (if needed), and file-based resources private to the extension.

Extensions will be versioned so that you can put out maintenance updates and feature updates. No action will need to be taken by the LiveCode user for maintenance updates, but the user will need to choose when to update LiveCode for feature updates.

Extensions can require that other extensions be installed and the IDE handles this seamlessly. If you load a stack requiring extensions that you don't have, the IDE will go and find them, but you might have to pay for some of them!

LiveCode Builder

LiveCode Builder is a variant of the existing LiveCode language designed to be a 'systems-building' language. It is a minimal language and all its functionality is notionally provided by libraries. Foreign code bindings are built in and they are statically compiled as bytecode.

One of the design goals of LiveCode Builder was the ease of translation to web-based technologies (JavaScript and HTML5). As LiveCode 8 matures, the plan is to move parts of the existing engine functionality into libraries written in LiveCode Builder, allowing most of the engine to be shared between HTML5 and traditional platforms. This is a key milestone on the journey to get HTML5 support.

How does LiveCode Builder code compare it with the current scripting language? For all the basics such as `repeat/if/switch/put`, it's much the same if not identical. The primary difference is that you have to specify the type for variables and instantiate them. Here is an example:

```
variable tArray as array
put the empty array into tArray
put "ben" into tArray["name"]
if tArray["name"] is "Ben" then
answer "I found" && tArray["name"]
end if
```

The other difference is that there is lots of new syntax to do things that previously weren't possible. For example, drawing a widget on screen accesses a canvas API. You also have to add some default setup to tell LiveCode what to do with the source file and what libraries to use. Here is a simple example of a pink circle widget:

```
widget com.livecode.extensions.beaumont.pinkCircle
metadata title is "My Pink Circle"
metadata author is "Benjamin Beaumont"
metadata version is "1.0.0"
use com.livecode.canvas
public handler OnPaint()
// Create a path with a radius of half the width of the canvas
variable tCirclePath as Path
put rounded rectangle path of my bounds with radius my height / 2 into
tCirclePath
// Set the paint to a solid pink color
set the paint of this canvas to solid paint with color [1, 0, 1]
// Fill the path
fill tCirclePath on this canvas
end handler
end widget
```

Additional constructs

Packages

A package defines the contents of an extension using a text file with a well-defined syntax. This description is passed to the LiveCode Builder compiler.

- Modular LiveCode source files (parts)
- Precompiled foreign code (code)
- Arbitrary file-based resources (file/folder)

Modules

A module is a collection of handlers composed of multiple source files specialized for specific platforms. Modules can be either widgets or libraries specified by the first line of the part...

♦ widget <name> [based on <name>]

♦ library <name> [for <platform>]

Roadmap

RunRev updates the LiveCode Roadmap about once a year. You can find the most recent one at:

```
http://livecode.com/community/roadmap/
```

LiveCode version 8.0 will encompass what we discussed previously and is the basis for many more advancements. The **Open Language** will be used to complete network, socket, and database libraries with English-like syntax as part of the development and testing process of this feature. **Widgets** will be the basis for improvement in controls to play videos across all platforms and a new vector shape object. A new **IDE** will be developed based on the previous technologies.

In August 2014, RunRev completed a $400k fund raising effort to add **HTML5** support to the LiveCode suite. The funding allowed the hiring of additional staff to support this effort. HTML5 web delivery will provide the ability to output your LiveCode applications into modern web browsers, allowing a faithful representation of your application within the browser environment. It uses HTML5 so it does not require a browser plugin. You will be able to author true web apps with LiveCode.

Several projects are queued for completion after this. A **Physics Engine** will incorporate Box2D into LiveCode along with an animation loop feature. A **Windows 8** port to support Windows mobile devices will be based on the new platform API developed for the Macintosh Cocoa port.

Index

G

General section, Standalone Application
   Settings option 184
Geometry Manager
   URL 91
   used, for positioning buttons 85
getPixel function
   testing 129
GitHub
   URL 221
Google Play
   about 31, 32
   URL 31
Google testing 204
GPS 160
Graphical User Interface (GUI) 166
Greenwich Mean Time (GMT) 157

H

handlers 10
hierarchy, LiveCode
   code 10
   stack structure 9
home card scripts
   about 173
   adding, to reminders app 173-176
HTML5 support 224
HTML content
   parsing, URL 109
HyperActive Software 200
HyperCard 2

I

iAd banner 217
Icons area, iOS section 188, 189
Icons Tools, iOS section 189
image
   selecting, for jigsaw puzzle 142
imageData
   about 128
   misusing 128
   transferring 146-149
image data format 126, 127

inspector palette
   used, in simple calculator application 14
installers
   creating, for Android 204
   creating, for iOS 200
interface controls
   about 23
   rollover buttons 24-26
   still image control 24
   Video player control 24
iOS
   app, preparing 197-199
   distribution certificate, creating for 207-210
   installers, creating for 200
   simulator used 56
   testing 56
iOS 8
   URL 74
iOS developer
   becoming 39-47
   iOS code names 48
   LiveCode membership, URL 40
   simulator, using 56
   URL 39, 40
   Xcode, installing 49, 50
iOS Provisioning Portal
   URL 58
iOS Release Notes
   URL 106
iOS SDKs
   LiveCode, pointing to 50
   URL 60
iOS section
   Basic Application Settings 187, 188
   Build for settings 186, 187
   Custom URL Scheme 191
   Icons area 188, 189
   Icons Tools 189
   Orientation Options 191
   Requirements and Restrictions options 192
   Splash Screens 190, 191
   Status Bar option 192
iPhone
   differerences, URL 86

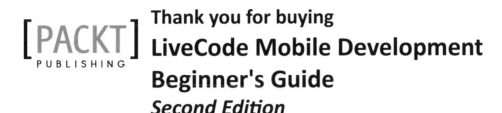

Thank you for buying
LiveCode Mobile Development Beginner's Guide
Second Edition

About Packt Publishing

Packt, pronounced 'packed', published its first book, *Mastering phpMyAdmin for Effective MySQL Management*, in April 2004, and subsequently continued to specialize in publishing highly focused books on specific technologies and solutions.

Our books and publications share the experiences of your fellow IT professionals in adapting and customizing today's systems, applications, and frameworks. Our solution-based books give you the knowledge and power to customize the software and technologies you're using to get the job done. Packt books are more specific and less general than the IT books you have seen in the past. Our unique business model allows us to bring you more focused information, giving you more of what you need to know, and less of what you don't.

Packt is a modern yet unique publishing company that focuses on producing quality, cutting-edge books for communities of developers, administrators, and newbies alike. For more information, please visit our website at www.PacktPub.com.

Writing for Packt

We welcome all inquiries from people who are interested in authoring. Book proposals should be sent to author@packtpub.com. If your book idea is still at an early stage and you would like to discuss it first before writing a formal book proposal, then please contact us; one of our commissioning editors will get in touch with you.

We're not just looking for published authors; if you have strong technical skills but no writing experience, our experienced editors can help you develop a writing career, or simply get some additional reward for your expertise.

LiveCode Mobile Development Beginner's Guide

ISBN: 978-1-84969-248-9   Paperback:246 pages

Create fun-filled, rich apps for Android and iOS with LiveCode

1. Create fun, interactive apps with rich media features of LiveCode.

2. Step-by-step instructions for creating apps and interfaces.

3. Dive headfirst into mobile application development using LiveCode backed with clear explanations enriched with ample screenshots.

LiveCode Mobile Development Cookbook

ISBN: 978-1-78355-882-7   Paperback:256 pages

90 practical recipes for creating cross-platform mobile applications with the power of LiveCode

1. Clear and concise tactics for cross-platform mobile applications with LiveCode.

2. Extend the capabilities of LiveCode with externals.

3. Discover advanced LiveCode features and techniques for app creation.

Please check **www.PacktPub.com** for information on our titles

LiveCode Mobile Development HOTSHOT

ISBN: 978-1-84969-748-4   Paperback:300 pages

Create your own exciting applications with 10 fantastic projects

1. Create your own mobile games and apps using LiveCode.

2. Develop user interfaces for mobile devices.

3. Use databases and advanced features of LiveCode.

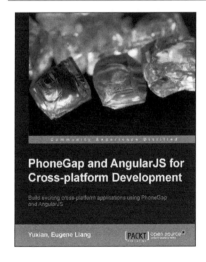

PhoneGap and AngularJS for Cross-platform Development

ISBN: 978-1-78398-892-1   Paperback:122 pages

Build exciting cross-platform applications using PhoneGap and AngularJS

1. Create a simple web-based app using AngularJS.

2. Build PhoneGap apps for iOS and Android with AngularJS, HTML, and CSS.

3. Learn how to use PhoneGap's command-line interface to build mobile applications using easy-to-follow, step-by-step exercises.

Please check **www.PacktPub.com** for information on our titles

Printed in Great Britain
by Amazon